Building Your Love Story
Developing Healthy Relationships

Marvin R. Barham, D. Min

Building Your Love Story:
Developing Healthy Relationships
Copyright 2015 JCI Publishing

All rights reserved under International and Federal Copyright Laws. Published in the United States by Jubilee Church International Publishing, North Little Rock, AR. Unauthorized reproduction is a violation of Federal Copyright Laws. For copies contact Jubilee Church International Ministries by visiting us at www.thejube.org or write us at 10321 Maumelle Blvd. North Little Rock, AR 72113. All Scripture taken from New King James Version (1982). Nashville, TN: Thomas Nelson Publishing. Used by permission. All rights reserved. Italics in original NKJV scriptures.

Table of Contents

Introduction 5

The Building Blocks of Relationship 13

Building Blocks of Family 33

Worldview of Relationship 65

Redefining Intimacy 103

Communication and Insecurities 121

Offenses and Forgiveness 143

Motives and Trust 161

Marriage Matters 181

Study and Discussion Questions 193

Bibliography 198

About the Author 205

Dedicated to
my amazing wife
Angie Barham

Introduction

It is still as vivid in my mind today as that night at six years old. I stood next to my mother looking into the night. We peered through the screen door into the backyard near the creek we loved to play in. We would catch crawdads and even water moccasin. But mother never knew about those. You could hear the water running in the background of his voice. There he was, as every night, since the sudden transformation. He used to scream and curse. He would spend most nights out drinking and gambling. But all of those memories are faint in the light of these nights. All you could see was the silhouette of him in the moon light on his knees, with hands lifted high into the air. It was as if he were trying to reach to the heavens and pull them down. Or maybe there was something he was trying to lift to the heavens. His voice was louder than when he used to get angry. But it was no longer filled with anger. Instead, it was filled with brokenness and passion like an intense longing or hunger.

I remember asking mom, "What is Dad doing?" She would reply, "He is seeking, praying, and crying out to God". After the intense seemingly hours of fervent cries, he would speak in a strange language. Then he began to speak in declarative authority as if he were commanding creation. Then it was back to more compassionate wailing and tears.

I never forgot those nights. They made an impression on me that shaped who I am today. They made a powerful impact in my youth when I strayed from the way. Those images, the demonstration of my father's intimacy with God, always led me home to my identity in Christ. I came to realize that my identity and greatest inheritance was this intimate relationship with my heavenly Father through Jesus Christ and the power of the Holy Spirit.

But it didn't end there. I was in the eighth grade when he spoke into my life that night at a little church outside of town. I was the typical little boy beginning to take interest in girls. You know; how you run up to a little girl at school and ask her if she will go steady with you. Then you ride away on your skateboard. But he began to speak about this girl I would like. How I would give my heart only to get it broken. Then he said I would meet a young girl through whom I would meet her best friend. It would be this one whom God had ordained and destined to be the one for the rest of my life. Well, what do you do with that in the eighth grade? So, I paid it no real attention. It wasn't until a few years later, when mother pulled out an old cassette tape. I know some of you may not even remember those. They were the newest technology following the eight track.

It had been three years since we had moved from that little town back to the city. Dad had a new church and I was now in high school. My focus was eating, weight lifting, and football. In those days, the thing to do most after school was to cruise around the park or hangout at the mall. It was there I met a little red headed girl from our rival school. We met at the mall on occasion and well, that was about the extent of the relationship. Until one day she tells me that she needs to date a guy who has a Trans Am. That was the cool car of the day. I was crushed. Really, how simple minded I thought. But I bounced back and was soon hanging out with a girl from the school dance team. We would see each other in passing to and from the art room; because the art instructor was also the drill team instructor. As a result, a lot of guys took art just to encounter the girls on the dance team.

By this time, my father had given me this old pickup truck. I would give anything to have that truck again today. It was a hard to find classic, a Ford Ranger XLT short wheel base. It had a Ford 360 engine with a Holley four barrel carburetor; with chrome pipes that made it rumble when you revved the engine. It had wood grain trim; an emerald green metallic paint job; tinted windows; leather seats; leather door panels; and a Kenwood stereo that you could hear a block away. And don't forget the sixty inch wide tires with chrome rims. It was a thing of beauty but cost a fortune to start.

I would swing by this girl's house, only to find some other guy there. I was never taught anything different than this whole cultural dating scheme. I began to realize there had to be a better way to find companionship for my future.

It was then that I met this girl's best friend. But for some reason I was scared to death to say anything to this girl. My mouth would just lockup; knees get weak; and stomach start to do things that were foreign to me. Occasionally, I would get the courage to say something stupid as we saw each other in the hallways or at a basketball game. But that was it. I did not know how to explain it or do anything about it.

Finally, football season started again. I loved football. I was not very large but fearless. I would take on the biggest dude on the field. I ran fast and hit hard. I played any position I could; Linebacker, halfback, punt team, kickoff team, anything to stay on that field. I had played football since peewee league. I had knocked out other guys' teeth, busted my head, their head and had broken my toes, fingers, and collar bone. But it wasn't long into the season when I seriously sprained my ankle and was on crutches.

I will never forget that night after the football game. I was in the locker room. My team mates were razing me about a young girl asking for me and waiting for me outside the locker room. You see, there was a dance that night at the school following the game. I had asked no one and was too afraid to ask her to the dance. Here I was on crutches and there she was waiting on me. I came hobbling out and down the steps. There she was. The lights from that football field just as well had been light from heaven as they shown on her beautiful face. Her countenance was that of an angel and I was awe struck and speechless.

"Hey. What ya doing?" This was the extent of conversation I could muster up. "Are you going to the dance?" I found enough courage to ask. Wow! What a goofball I must have been. "Well, I don't know," she said. "It depends on if someone is ever going to ask me to go." Today I can see the strength and tenacity of leadership that was there that night in my wife. Well, to the dance we went and eventually I asked her out on a date.

What did I know about romance and relationship? I was just a kid. I had no concept of long term, eternal, covenant relationship. What I did have was a healthy fear of the Lord; a simple understanding of commitment from my parents who had made it through tough times; and a fundamental concept of who I was in Christ.

The night of that first date, I picked her up in my pickup truck. I had been practicing driving with my left hand and my right arm resting on the back of the seat. I picked her up and had planned to take her to Red Lobster. It was the newest fancy restaurant in town. I had saved up and was going to really impress her. Instead, she suggested we go to Wendy's Hamburgers and get a salad. I thought, "Wow! Lord, this has got to be the one! She has got her priorities right!" We pull in and park. I turned to her and said, "This might be strange and you might think I'm crazy but I need you to listen to this cassette tape before we continue in this relationship."

Between the dance and this date my mother had pulled out that cassette tape of my father prophesying to me back in eighth grade. She said to me, "Son, I think you need to listen to this." Thank God for mothers like mine who hang on to the words of the Lord for their children. I listened and sure enough, he was right on. He had said, "You will meet this red headed girl and you will be heartbroken. You will meet another who will be on a cheer squad or something. But she will not be the one for your life. However, through her, you will meet her best friend." He went on to describe her down to her physical appearance and the history of her life.

So, here we are in the parking lot of Wendy's listening to my father three years earlier prophesying about us and this very moment. He began by praying in his spiritual language and then began to speak of each young lady. Then he began to speak of her. I thought she was going to bolt out of that truck, run and call her father to come get her. The only assurances I had was that 1.) God had spoken this and; 2.) Before I even knew who she was her father had attended my father's church a couple of times where my father had ministered to him personally. So, I thought to myself, "Maybe, just maybe, this will not freak her out too bad."

That night after dinner and a movie, we went back to my parent's home. There my parents ministered inner healing, through words of knowledge, to her about everything in her life. Sometime later I had the privilege of leading my wife to Christ on the beach in Pensacola, FL. We stuck together for seven years while she waited for me to finish high school and my first four years of college. We were married in November of 1991. Shortly thereafter, I left for Infantry, Airborne and Air Assault schools.

From that day forward we vowed to honor God with our relationship and future. We consecrated every part of our lives: every day, each moment, every struggle, every joy was God's no matter what. We vowed to die to self and always honor and prefer the other above ourselves. We vowed to respect one another and never raise our voices or let the sun go down on our anger. We vowed to be content and good stewards, trusting God with whatever and all that He gave us.

Thirty years and five children later, we have been through some great times as well as some tough times together. We have grieved and mourned together. We have laughed and rejoiced together and we have stuck together as a team through it all. We share everything and the affection is as alive and rich today as ever. That night at the dance, I was on crutches and had to lean on her to dance. To this day, I cannot dance without her. I still lean on her every day. Together we cling to our Savior. We have grown in Christ together and shared the greatest joys that one could ever ask for in this life.

We have learned real, true, sacred, intimate relationship through our love for the Father.

This is what this book is about; How to find and live in true, pure, and perfect relationship with God the Father through His Son Jesus Christ; How to honor Him in every relationship He has blessed you with in this life. It is to strengthen your marriage; your family; and mold your children into the relational image of the Father. It is to redeem that which is sacred - relationship.

The Building Blocks of Relationship

There are many things being taught in the church today from healing to prosperity. As I sought the Lord, I began to ask God what it is that we need to understand in order to be stronger and healthier as a people. What do we need to understand in order to pursue Him deeper and be the Bride that He is returning for?

I am amazed that in the Body of Christ we have all types of revelation, programs, and ministries going on. Yet, often the thing the Church continues to struggle with most is relationship. We can have all kinds of ministries and be successful in our ministries, but if we fail at relationship, we have missed the intent of God. The very nature and essence of God is relationship. If He is not all that you need; if the portion of His relationship and love He has extended to us is not enough, then nothing in this life will be enough. There will always be an emptiness and void. The Bible tells us that it is His love, His Word, and this relationship that God has with all creation, that keeps and sustains it all. The only reason the stars remain in the heavens is because of His love and relationship to them. The only reason the earth and all creation continues to function and exist is because of this relationship and the authority of it therein. If this love and relationship is enough to keep the stars in the heavens and hold all creation together, then it has got to be enough to meet my every need. It has got to be enough to fill the void in my soul. If not, then the problem is not in God's relationship to me but my relationship to Him. I have found the only things of any value in this world, which I will leave behind, are the relationships throughout my life. My stuff will fade away, be sold, or the government will take it. The only things I will leave of any significance are relationships. In this life, God has given me just enough time to make the most of those relationships and glorify Him. I have found that the true meaning of life is this: It is a sovereign and privileged journey to know God.

The most valuable gift that you can give to anyone is your time. Never take it for granted. It is a priceless commodity. Learn to live with the motivation that all of your life is an opportunity to grow deeper in relationship with God and provoke others to the same. In each relationship, learn to listen to the motives of people's heart and to know them after the Spirit of Christ. Each moment you have with people, seek to make the most of it, treasure it, value them and the time you have with them. During that time seek to build relationship God's way. In order to build any relationship God's way, Christ must be at the core of that relationship. If Christ is not at the core of the relationship, then the relationship will never experience the depth of God's intent. For Christ to be the core, He must be Lord.

Deuteronomy 7:6-9, "For you are a holy people to the Lord your God; the Lord your God has chosen you to be a people for Himself, a special treasure above all the peoples on the face of the earth. The Lord did not set His love on you nor choose you because you were more in number than any other people, for you were the least of all peoples; but because the Lord loves you, and because He would keep the oath which He swore to your fathers, the Lord has brought you out with a mighty hand, and redeemed you from the house of bondage, from the hand of Pharaoh king of Egypt. Therefore know that the Lord your God, He is God, the faithful God who keeps covenant and mercy for a thousand generations with those who love Him and keep His commandments."

God has called you to be a holy people. Have you ever heard someone say, "I'm not perfect; God is not finished with me yet"? On one hand, I understand that people mean they are still learning to grow in Christ. On the other hand, it remains, at its root, a statement of justification for not living as Christ. The work God began in you He finished at the cross. When He hung on that tree, he said, "It is finished." In Christ you became a "new creature." It is not so much that God is working on you but that God wants you to work on you or to do your part of reciprocating the relationship by allowing the completion of the transformation of your heart and mind. What we often do is put the responsibility for change off on God. We seek to negate the responsibility that is given us. I am amazed at how people often go through multiple relationships, jobs, and church memberships and have a victim mentality. It was always the other person that was the problem in the relationship; it was "those people" who caused them to have to be called by God to leave that church. Yet, they never come to the revelation that the only common denominator in each relationship, each job conflict, and each church change was them. Also, they always find a way to involve God somehow and place the responsibility on Him.

Let me share with you the process of divine fulfillment in a person's life. The promises of God do

Copyright 2014 Marvin Barham, D. Min

not come without a change in our lives, from living by our supreme selfishness to His supreme sovereignty. Change does not come without conflict with our fleshly nature that must be crucified with Christ. Conflict must be resolved by the revelation of God's grace that comes from a place of solitude through personal introspection in light of His great love. Joseph did not understand his purpose in God's promise until he dealt with his heart in a prison, even though he was unjustly placed there. Abraham, Moses, Joshua, Elijah, John the Baptist and Jesus all experienced the true wonders of God first in a wilderness before walking in the fullness of their identity. So, no matter what, stay positive. Consider the alternative. Regardless of the circumstances, you cannot fulfill your purpose in His promises without His favor. You disqualify yourself with your attitude and perspective if not surrendered to His will and His way. Your relationship with God is less about where you attend church and how much Scripture you can quote. It's more about your obedience and honor to His way of relationship. God is not looking for your affiliation to Him but the affirmation of your relationship with Him. Ben Sprouse states, "When Christ asks you to follow Him, the implication is that you let Him lead."

You are called to be a part of a holy people unto the Lord your God. What does it mean to be holy in God? It means to be surrendered to God. It means to be an obedient people. It means to be a people fashioned after the image of God. In Deuteronomy 7:6, the word "holy" is *qadowsh* קָדוֹשׁ meaning set apart, sacred, and consecrated or belonging only to and for that which is Holy. To say, "Well, I am only human," is a lame excuse and to make the sacrifice of Christ of no avail. Christ has redeemed you and made you a new creature. You are, therefore, a new man, or a new woman and in that you think differently, act differently, choose differently, speak differently, respond differently and love differently. As well, you have to view everything differently including relationships. You must view every relationship through the eyes of God. God has chosen you to be a special people unto Himself among all people who are on the face of the earth. What is it that makes you special? In Deuteronomy 7:7, God says that He did not choose them because they were more in number, but because He "loves them." God chose to love you not because you were talented, good looking, or born of good stock. There is no other reason that God loves you, except that He chose to love you and chooses to love you every day.

In Deuteronomy, God tells them that He brought them out and redeemed them from the house of bondage. With that, He keeps His oaths and has brought you out of the slavery of sin. Jesus said, in John 8:34, "Most assuredly, I say to you, whoever commits sin is a slave to sin." The Apostle Paul tells us in Romans 11:30, Ephesians 2:3, Ephesians 5:8, and Titus 3:3 that you once were a slave bound by the flesh but Christ has set you free. Without Christ in your life, you live a supremely selfish life, void of divine purpose and identity, rebellious to the sovereign will and way of the

Lord. God delivered you through the love of Christ who gave all of Himself to show you how to have relationship. God is a God of relationship. God is a faithful God who keeps His covenant. Deuteronomy 7:9, God commands you to "know" that God is God; a faithful God who keeps "covenant" and "mercy" with those who reciprocate His love and keep His commandments. In this, we find the building blocks, the cement, the nails, the nuts, the bolts, the glue, the frame work of that which holds relationships together. If you learn these, you can grow faithful in Christ and right relationship. You have to truly "know" God. You have to be faithful. You have to understand covenant. You have to give mercy. You have to keep your word. You have to have a steadfast love.

Jeremiah 24:5-7, ""Thus says the LORD, the God of Israel: 'Like these good figs, so will I acknowledge those who are carried away captive from Judah, whom I have sent out of this place for [their own] good, into the land of the Chaldeans. 'For I will set My eyes on them for good, and I will bring them back to this land; I will build them and not pull [them] down, and I will plant them and not pluck [them] up. 'Then I will give them a heart to know Me, that I [am] the LORD; and they shall be My people, and I will be their God, for they shall return to Me with their whole heart."

If your heart is upright before Him, then He is looking out for your good and His glory. God wants to build you up, not tear you down. God wants to establish you and to give you a heart to know the Lord your God.

God wants to build a relationship where you may be intimate with His heart; that you may have an intimate knowledge of His heart; that you may intimately experience, encounter and embrace the heart of Father God. God wants your whole heart in this relationship. Not half of it; not fragments; not bits and pieces that you choose to loan Him.

The God of the Bible is a God of relationship. He views relationship as covenantal, eternal, family, sacred and intimate. Even in the church, too many people have a view of relationship from a pagan, humanistic, narcissistic, hedonistic and unbiblical worldview. Most of our views of relationship have been shaped and developed by the relationships that our parents had or failed to have; by broken relationships or disappointments in our lives and the lives of those around us; and by the influence of the secular world we live in.

We must learn to view relationship the way God views relationship. As such, throughout Scripture, we find three building blocks of relational development: 1.) Relationship with God; 2.) Relationship with Family; 3.) Relationship with Others. The first of these building blocks is a relationship with God. All other relationships must be built upon this relationship. All other relationships flow out of this relationship. This relationship must be the cornerstone from which all other relationships are built. This relationship is foundational. To have relationship with anyone else, and the relationship with God not be the foundation, means that you cannot share the most important part of your life and who you are with the other person without making your relationship with God second in your life. God will not take the back seat while you drive or let someone else drive the relationships of your life. When you build a house, there has to be good and solid soil. Then you have to lay a good foundation. Without a good foundation on solid ground, that which you build will not stand. The earth is going to shift, the cold, heat and storms are going to come. If your foundation is not solid, you will end up with cracks in the foundation and the structure will eventually fall apart. When you lay the foundation, you first lay the cornerstone which determines how the whole house will be built. It determines if it is square and level. Once you build a house on a foundation that is not square or level, all of your floors, walls, windows, doors, everything will be crooked. You then find you are continually trying to compensate to make things fit and work together. Your boards are all different lengths. You begin to bend boards and put tension or pressure on them to try and make them join together; all of this because you started out wrong. This is exactly the way many people live their lives in relationships. They are constantly struggling through all kinds of crisis and drama in their lives, constantly having to compromise and compensate in their relationship with God, and trying to fit all things together because they started it all out wrong and the cornerstone was not first laid in their lives.

Therefore, the first building block of right relationship must be your relationship with Jesus Christ. You will always have relational issues and dysfunction until Jesus Christ is the cornerstone and your first and most important relationship.

You must have God's perspective of relationship to you and you to others. God views relationship as covenantal, as family and as eternal. He keeps His covenant and mercy for a thousand generations (Deuteronomy 7:9; 1 Chronicles 16:15; Psalm 105:8). Relationships are eternal, both good ones and bad ones. If you were responsible for botching a relationship and never attempted to reconcile because of your own pride or unwillingness to repent, then when you stand before God you will account for that relationship. You might think, "When I get to heaven, I am going to see Grandma again and all of those wonderful friends that went before me." But when you get there, you will see them possibly even among those relationships that you failed to reconcile with. And God will ask, "What did you do to try and reconcile, to bring healing and life in these relationships or did you just toss those relationships aside?" We don't like to consider that. In our hearts and minds we have justified that we had issues with those people; don't have to see them again; and don't have to speak to them. We de-friended them on Facebook and they left our church so we have no more responsibility to that relationship. When you stand before God, that relationship is just as eternal as those good relationships you hope to see again someday in glory. It always amazes me how we value so many things but value relationships so little. I'll never forget the time a young man called me and said, "Pastor, I came home and found that my wife had left me and took everything! Why, she even took my television! How am I going to watch NASCAR now?" I said, "Brother, you mean your wife and kids are gone and the thing you are most concerned with is your television?" He replied, "But Pastor, I had that TV before we were even married and there is a race on tonight."

God's view of relationship must be what the church is built on and not individual opinions, feelings, not even personal wants or needs. The church will never be all she is meant to be and will never know the true power of her strength until we get this building block of relationship down. Many people today view their relationship with God, unfortunately, as something less than real and tangible. Partly because much of the church has doctrinally propagated that God is not real and tangible, therefore, your doctrine justifies your sinful nature. You simply go to church, sing a song, drop something in the offering plate, if you are up to it, and hit the door unchanged. God wants you to encounter Him and His love. The Holy Spirit is real and tangible. His Word and His love are real and tangible. We can touch them and see them working and operating, giving real hope and real life through those who truly know Him. You don't need "Doctor Feel Good" or "O'Pray to Any God." It is the power of God flowing through you and me to form a right and intimate relationship. That is the hope of His glory in the earth that mankind is longing for in their souls. Relationship with God alone gives real and eternal hope and life. You do not need a psychiatrist, psychologist, daytime soap, morning show reports or a television talk show host to tell you how to have right relationship. God already has. And God's way is not theory but is proven from the foundations of the earth. God has given you the tools to have a right relationship. God's jealousy is not anthropomorphic (relating to human nature) but is holy. He is jealous (like a bride for her husband to be monogamous) for that which is rightfully His through covenant.

Some perceive a deep relationship with God as unobtainable, cold, distant and lacking in emotional connectedness. Many do not have understanding of what real relationship with God looks like and it is reflected in their relationship with others. If you cannot see and understand what a real relationship with God looks like, then you will struggle with having healthy relationship with others. This is why the world has to see, through us, how to have right relationship. If the church does not get this right then our efforts are in vain. The greatest thing we can do to reach the lost is to truly learn to love one another as Christ loved us. Jesus said, "By this all will know that you are My disciples, if you have love for one another" (John 13:35).

We live in a time and culture where, even in the church, relational dysfunction seems to be accepted as the new normal. In the Disney-Pixar movie *The*

Incredibles, those who have special super hero powers have been forced to remain undisclosed and integrate into the general public to live as "normal families." In one particular scene, the husband is dealing with the anxiety of his job and the suppression of his true passion while the mother contends with the out of control kids at the dinner table. Screaming for intervention from the husband, the mother tells the children that they cannot disclose their hero identities and must do their best to just be a normal family. The eldest child replies, "Normal? What does anyone in this family know about normal? The only normal one is Jack-Jack, and he's not even toilet trained."

Do not be a Christian in hiding. Do not hide your relationship with your God that you might fit in with the rest of the world by their definition of normal. In Matthew 10:32, Jesus says, ""Therefore whoever confesses Me before men, him I will also confess before My Father who is in heaven." And in Romans 1:16, the Apostle Paul states, "For I am not ashamed of the gospel of Christ, for it is the power of God to salvation for everyone who believes…" As Christians, we have succumbed to a culture that has tried to oppress the greatest gift God has given you. We try to be normal as the world continually seeks to redefine what is relationally normal. As our families fall to pieces, we have accepted dysfunction as the new normal. Everyone in the family is doing their own thing, going different directions and there is not real relationship. The only relationship we have are the 400 people we call our friends on Facebook or Twitter, most of whom we have no idea of the connection. And if they don't "like" or "comment" on our posts then we are devastated. The first thing we want to do is "de-friend" somebody. If we are "in a relationship" and that relationship is ended, we are less concerned about the relationship and more concerned about making sure our "status" is up to date; I've gone from "In a relationship" to "Single". And now there is a new category called "It's Complicated". That's just what we needed.

If you are in a godly relationship that was ordained by God, defined by God, and destined by God, because you have surrendered your romance to God, then when it falls apart and your greatest concern is changing your Facebook status, that is a clue something is seriously wrong with your view of relationship. What needs to change is not your status. You may be posting Scriptures and quotes from other people's intimacy with God to show others the depth of relationship you have with God, but you are not fooling God.

To know God is to be intimate with God. Dr. Douglas Wheeler states, "You can have knowledge of God but not be intimate with God." In his book Betrothed: *An Intimate Face-to-Face Walk with God*, Dr. Douglas Wheeler uses three Hebrew words to illustrate a life-transforming understanding of what it means to know God intimately. We will begin in Genesis 4:1 where it says that Adam knew his wife Eve again and she bore him a son. The word "knew" here in the Hebrew is yada'' יָדַע and it means to learn to know;

to see; to experience; confess; acknowledge; to be revealed. In context, it means be intimate with God as a groom and bride. There is only one way for a man to "know" his wife and her be impregnated and that is to be intimate (Wheeler 2012). It is the same context used when Jesus says in Matthew 7:23 that there will be those who stand before Him and boast of all their great works of ministry and He will declare to them, "I never knew you; depart from Me, you who practice lawlessness!" In this passage, the Greek word is *ginosko* γινώσκω meaning to learn; gain knowledge of; feel; understand; Jewish idiom for sexual intercourse between a man and a woman. So, Jesus is saying, "Depart from Me because we never had an intimate relationship." Do not be the one who boasts of being on the worship team; of how accurate you can prophecy; of your success as a pastor in building up your congregation and yet stand before Him only to hear Him say, "We were never intimate."

The result or fruit of Adam's intimacy was that it produced life. This is the pattern of relationship that God has created you for. If you have right relationship with the cornerstone, with God, and there is an intimate relationship, then there should be fruit of that relationship and it should be life giving. If you have intimate relationship with God, then the fruit of your life should not be destructive, tearing down, murmuring, complaining, gossiping, tale bearing, not backbiting, filled with envy, jealousy or resentment. For the fruit of the Spirit in Christ Jesus is love, joy, peace, longsuffering, kindness, goodness, faithfulness, gentleness and self-control (Galatians 5:22-23). For the fruit of the Spirit is in all goodness, righteousness and truth (Ephesians 5:9).

Your relationship with God shapes and defines how you view relationship with others. It is less about other people's issues or dysfunction and more about yours; it is about your issues; your dysfunction and your relationship with God. When God chose to have relationship with you, with all mankind, you had issues. You were as dysfunctional as they come. You were a sinner, rebellious, selfish, and full of pride. You were rejecting Him, spitting on him and yet He loved you. He did not blame the problems in the relationship on you. Instead, He said I will take it all. I will take the blame, the sin, the hurt, the dysfunction upon myself and kill it for you.

There is another Hebrew word for the phrase or idiom "to know" and it is the word *da'ath* דעת which is a similar word to *yada'* but also means "to get to know", "to become acquainted", and "to acquire greater knowledge of". It leads to *yada'* יָדַע intimacy in that you seek to increase the level of intimacy in the relationship by a continual discovery of the one in the relationship that you may learn their heart's motives and intents. It is to know them after the depth of their heart; to perceive, discern, and understand them in the wisdom of God after the Spirit and not after the flesh. In this understanding of relationship, a longing for the fellowship and relationship is created. And grace grows in the relationship.

We live in a culture today where people not only speed date but they will meet each other online one day then meet that night to have sex. We have perverted intimacy to the point of just send me a picture and see how attractive you are and if I want to have sex with you. But have so many not taken the same mentality with God? If He stimulates me or can make me an attractive offer I might give Him a try? Does the church not continually seek to make God more appealing and attractive to those who live by the flesh and have no desire to exchange their sinful nature for that of a redeemed identity in Christ? Do we not say to God, "I have talked to you once or twice, Lord. I even made it to church five times this year. And now God, I am in a crisis and need to have an intimate encounter with you to get me through the moment."

You see, suddenly when we need something, we want to experience His intimacy but skip the requirement or necessity to get to know Him. You need to become acquainted with Him beyond a familiarity. You need to spend time with Him and learn to love what He loves; know what breaks His heart and what brings Him joy; to get to know His desires and passions. You have to reach the point in the relationship with God where you have a desire to acquire greater knowledge and understanding of Him. In *da'ath*, you seek to increase the level of intimacy in the relationship by continual discovery of the one you are in relationship with; that you might know them after the depth of their heart's motives and intent. In this understanding of relationship, a longing for the fellowship in the relationship is created and grace grows in the relationship.

Finally, to truly know God you must learn to *'ahabah* אהבה God. It means to love, but in a deeper and intimate sense of the word, as Jacob loved Rachel in Genesis 29:20. Dr. Wheeler states, that in the Hebrew, it is more than a word but it is described as a sound like the sound of panting (*'arag* עָרַג). As David said in Psalm 42:1, "As the deer pants for the water brooks; so pants my soul for You, O God." It is like a big buck deer running from the hunter who just shot and missed. This deer, with his big rack, almost lost his life and now he is running as fast as he can to find a place of safety. He runs as far and as fast as he can, but now he is thirsty, so he runs to the nearest brook and begins to lap it up with his heart pounding. In between, he stops to breathe. You can almost hear his hard and fast breathing and beating of his heart through the entire woods. This is *'ahabah*. This is a picture of the longing that God desires for us to have for Him daily. It is a deep thirst for life sustaining desire for the person and presence of God with all of our heart, soul and strength. This is the depth of relationship that God has for you. This is the value of relationship that God longs for you to have with your brothers and sisters in the Body of Christ and in your family. All relationship has to begin with desire, then a searching and discovery, before there can be true and pure intimacy.

If you can learn to *yada'* God, *da'ath* God, and *'ahabah* God, then you can know how to have strong and healthy relationships with other people; you can know how to build lifelong relationships with your children and teach them how to build healthy relationships in their lives; you can know how to build and restore relationships with your husband or wife; you can know how to restore broken relationships of the past. It is in this depth of relationship with God that you can even learn to love your enemies. How do you think Jesus expected you to love your enemies? The same way He did, through His intimate relationship with the Father. You can love even those who persecute you in the midst of your hurt when you truly learn to *yada', da'ath,* and *'ahabah* God. The love of Christ was not dictated by others but by His love for the Father.

How can you love one another as Christ commanded if you don't even want to get to know one another or you do not avail yourself for fellowship and relationship building? You have to make relationship building by God's definition a priority in your life. You were fashioned after the love of the Father. You cannot truly say you love your neighbor if you have no sincerity to know them, their heart, hurts, or needs.

Do you long to know God? Maybe you have never experienced this depth and level of relationship with God. Maybe you have never understood God beyond a religious idea but you desire to have that intimate encounter that transforms your identity in Christ. Cry out to Him today and just tell Him how you long for Him. If you call on Him, He is faithful to answer your call and fill you with His intimate presence.

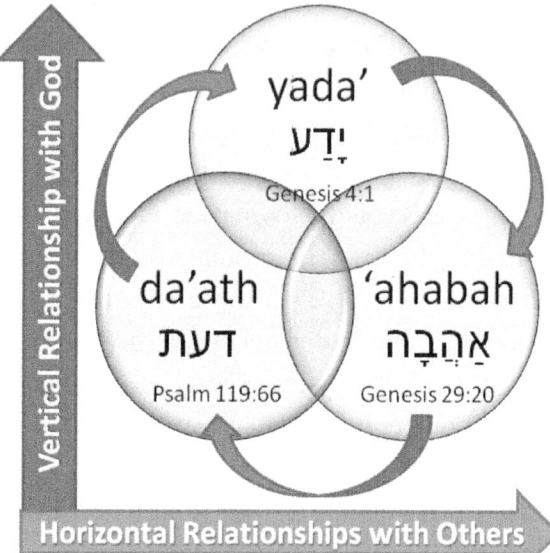

da'ath: יָדַע *yada'* (primitive root)

Copyright 2014 Marvin Barham, D. Min
ahabah, da'ath, yada process: (Wheeler 2012)

Building Blocks of Family

Proverbs 4:1 says, "Hear, my children, the instruction of a father, and give attention to know understanding." Galatians 4:6 says, "And because you are sons, God has sent forth the Spirit of His Son into your hearts, crying out, 'Abba, Father!'" Abba αββα is a Greek word meaning father. We are crying "Father, Father." The intent is the expression of deeper intimacy more than a mere religious connotation. In days of old, there were not many who had that form of intimacy with God as a Father other than those instances such as Abraham, Moses, Joshua, David and select others. The word Abba was only used by a child to express a pure and innocent affection to their father. So, the cry here is a cry of intimacy to know Father God as a child of God. Thus Jesus says in Luke 16-17, "…Let the little children come to Me, and do not forbid them; for of such is the kingdom of God. Assuredly, I say to you, whoever does not receive the kingdom of God as a little child will by no means enter it." You must enter His Kingdom through intimate relationship.

This goes back to having that desire for God. God desires for His children to have the desire for affectionate and intimate relationship with Him. As in any relationship, there has to be a mutual desire. I can desire to know you and build relationship with you but if you have no desire to know or build relationship with me, the relationship will go no further than acquaintance. I can simply say I know of you because we met once. Unfortunately, this is the depth of relationship that many have with God. They know of Him because they met Him once. The sad thing is that many are satisfied with that level of relationship with God or they have been taught that this is all there is. We must reciprocate the desire for relationship with God. All relationship begins with desire and if we ever lose that desire, often the relationship begins to weaken. That desire has to be built on something stronger than emotion or physical attraction. This is why the idea of "falling" in love is not a biblical concept. I typically associate falling with accidents that result in pain. Therefore, if you can "fall" into love you can probably fall out of love as well. Love with God is not an accident. God first chose to love you. God did not choose to love you for anything you were or could do for Him. He chose to love you because God is love. The desire for God to love you is already there. You do not have to do anything to try and get God to desire love for you. He already loves you and desires to have relationship with you. His desire to love you has been there since the foundations of the earth and it is unshakable. The problem is that you have to have the desire to love Him. You and I need an unchangeable, unshakable, mature love and constant desire for God. God desires us to know Him after the Spirit of God and not after our flesh. Thus, "God is Spirit, and those who worship Him must worship in spirit and truth."

This desire cannot be a fleshly, superficial desire where I am in the relationship to get what I can get out of it for myself. But it is a desire (*'ahabah*) that leads to a continual discovery (*da'ath*). Once I have a true and sincere desire for God, the more I begin to pursue God. When I begin to seek Him with my whole heart, I begin to discover God. In Jeremiah 29:13, God says, "And you will seek Me and find [Me], when you search for Me with all your heart." In this discovery, I find the heart of Father; I discover His will, His intent, His purpose for my life; I discover His nature, His character, and the depth of His love, mercy and grace. I then find myself in a place of intimacy (*yada'*) with the one whom my soul doth love (Song of Songs 3:4, "…I found the one I love. I held him and would not let him go…"). This is why, if you skip pure, sincere desire and you skip discovery and try to go straight to intimacy, you pervert the relationship.

This principle applies to romantic relationships, your spiritual relationships and even your relationship in family. God's desire for intimate relationship is rooted in family. He is father and we are to be His sons and daughters. As sons and daughters, we are not orphans or foster children who cannot or are afraid to develop deep rooted relationship, but we have been adopted and are truly free to sincerely know Him.

The church is supposed to be the example of family in the image of God. The church is supposed to be the example of perfect relationship through Christ Jesus; the demonstration of right relationship through perfect love; the bride and the groom. In John 13:35, Jesus says, "By this, all will know that you are my disciples, if you have love for one another." Instead, the church too often seems to be the most dysfunctional when it comes to relationships today. There is more offense, backbiting, gossiping, tale bearing, fighting, and strife than in the night clubs. More people are wounded and hurt in the church than in the average office environment. Christians have devalued friendship. They will kick a friendship to the curb in a heartbeat if they get offended or do not want to be held accountable. There is no real depth of relationship that binds us to one church family or another. We have even developed rational justifications so we can easily move from one church to another when we get easily offended or have gotten all we feel we can out of that group of people. We have justified all sorts of relational dysfunction leaving souls wounded and fragmented.

Only in Christianity and Judaism is God referred to as "Father". You never hear of a Buddhist, Hindu or Muslim refer to their god(s) as "Father." Only Yahweh (YHVH יהוה) is Father. Only the God of Abraham, Isaac and Jacob is a personable God who desires personal relationship.

The word Father denotes that there is more than being the one who produces offspring but one who imparts, corrects and guides, encourages and instructs in life. Father denotes one who has relationship with His children. Therefore, if you do not have relationship with Him, He is probably not your Father. I hear preachers, politicians, and Christians of all sorts say, "We are all God's children." That is not what the Scripture tells me. We may all be God's creation but we are not all God's children. Ephesians 5:8 says, "For you were once darkness, but now you are light in the Lord. Walk as children of light." And 1 John 3:10 states, "In this the children of God and the children of the devil are manifest: Whoever does not practice righteousness is not of God, nor is he who does not love his brother." In Matthew 13:38, Jesus speaks of the sons of the Kingdom opposed to the sons of the wicked one. The difference between the wheat and tare is that one bears fruit of the relationship and the other does not. What "fellowship" (*chabar* חָבַר: unity; alliance) does light have with darkness? (2 Corinthians 6:14- "Do not be unequally yoked together with unbelievers. For what fellowship has righteousness with lawlessness? And what communion has light with darkness?"). Your relationship with God is defined by the life you live and the choices you make. You either reflect His authority and influence in your life or you're continuing to live by supreme selfishness. You either live by the redemption He has secured for you through grace or you live by your own will through rebellion and religious justification, void of relationship. It has been said that religion is rules without relationship and rituals without righteousness.

Father denotes the very nature of who God is. God is a God of relationship. Man was created to glorify God. The way God is glorified is through your relationship with Him and your relationship with others. His value of relationship with you was demonstrated at the cross. It is this demonstration of relationship that must be at the heart of family relationships.

Foundational Principles of Fathering

Proverbs 4:1-5

- Instruction in the ways of wisdom
- Disciplines in obedience
- Impartation of knowledge
- Impression of understanding
- Reverence and honor of divine authority
- Application of godly wisdom

Silvey, Mark. *The Proverbs Plan for Family Discipleship* (2010). Parker, KS: Hearts of the Fathers. Copyright 2014 Marvin Barham, D. Min

There are six foundational principles of relationship established by fathers. The father is supposed to exemplify the prophet, priest and king of his household. If you are single, then God is your father and husband. If you are single with children, then you have to walk in both roles as both father and mother. However, you do not have to go it alone. In the family of God, there should be spiritual fathers who exemplify the roles of prophet, priest, and king to you and your children. Therefore, if you are so blessed to have godly leaders who exemplify such godly character and attributes, it means you have to actually show up to church for your children to be influenced by such leaders. Skipping church and sleeping in while the kids watch cartoons does nothing for the relational dysfunction, regardless of how great the leaders of your church may be.

In the Old Testament the prophet gave the word of the Lord. He taught others how to hear and follow the instruction of the Lord. The priest led the people to repentance and lived a life in demonstration of consecration before the Lord. He led the people in worship to God. The King demonstrated the governing authority of God and how important it was to live by the Law of the Lord. It is in these principles that we are to father and lead our families in relationship with God and relationship one with another.

There are six foundational principles established for fathers in Scripture regarding family. We find these in Proverbs 4:1-5, "Hear, my children, the instruction of a father, and give attention to know understanding; for I give you good doctrine: Do not forsake my law. When I was my father's son, tender and the only one in the sight of my mother, He also taught me, and said to me: 'Let your heart retain my words; Keep my commands, and live. Get wisdom and gain understanding! Do not forget, nor turn away from the words of my mouth.'" The first foundational principle is instructing in the ways of wisdom; teaching them how to know, defend, and live in truth. Biblical Wisdom can be defined as the ability to make godly choices in life. This wisdom only has authority where it is applied and adhered to. Another definition is the ability to see the relationship between the problems of life and the principles of Scripture that have been violated. The second is discipline in obedience. This is learning how to pray, fast, seek and serve the Lord. In this, they learn self-restraint, self-control, respect, honor, values, priorities and much more. Teach them discipline in prayer, fasting and to seek the Lord from their early childhood. Then with other families doing the same, you will have fewer behavioral disciplinary problems in the future. The third is impartation of knowledge: the disciplines in the study of Scripture and the principle of God. Fourth is impression of understanding. To make an impression means to leave a permanent image on something. We do this by teaching them how to seek, discern, and know sound revelation of God and His Word and how to worship God with their whole life. The fifth principle is reverence and honor of divine authority through love, correction, growth and the development of maturity.

And sixth is the application of godly wisdom. This means teaching them through demonstration, how to live it from the heart and connect with God through relationship. You can have all the others but if you do not have the last one, you are missing the whole point. It is all about teaching our children how to have relationship with God. If you're relationally dysfunctional with God, do not expect anything better from your children. If you are relationally dysfunctional in the church, then church will probably not be a priority in your children's lives either. If you are relationally dysfunctional as a husband and father, then your children will probably be relationally dysfunctional in like manner (Silvey 2010)

These principles do not apply to just fathers but to mothers and single parents as well. In fact, they apply to all of us in the Body of Christ.

You know why God created man before He created the woman? Some ladies might like to think it was because God wanted to see the mistakes then correct them all when He perfected His creation with woman. But I heard a minister say one time that it was because God wanted to first instruct Adam how to lead his family through the Spirit of God. Once God saw that Adam was functioning correctly through the image (through the authority and dominion of holy relationship that God had given him) only then did God say to Adam, "You are now qualified to have a woman."

There are a lot of men who either have a good woman or want one. As well, there are women who have or want a good man. In either case, God wants you qualified. All too often, the things we think qualify us, or qualify a good man or woman, are not the same as God's perspective. God does not judge after the appearances of men but after the heart. What are God's qualifications? "But the fruit of the Spirit is love, joy, peace, longsuffering, kindness, goodness, faithfulness, gentleness, self-control" (Galatians 5:22-23). You need to know how to have right relationship; handle difficult situations; stewardship; godly wisdom; discernment; sound judgment; and have a job. You need to know how to know the will of God; rightly divide the Word of God; teach it to your family; be free from perversion; be free of selfish childishness; and trust God as your provider. You need to know how to handle conflict and resolve relational issues in peace and life; you need to know how to discipline your children in the admonition of the Lord; you need to know how to die to sin and self and lay your life down for others preferring them above yourself; you need to know how to walk and lead a family after the Spirit, truth, and righteousness of the Lord that you might be qualified. Stop expecting God to bring someone else into your life just so their life can be as big a mess as yours. God is not looking to bring someone into your life so you can goof up their life too. Instead, God first wants to see you walking in maturity and stability so that He can use you to bring out the best of Him in someone else. I believe God may have said to

Adam, "Do you think you are ready to bring out the best in the best thing I have made yet?"

In Genesis 1:26 God said that we were created in His image (צלם *tselem*) and likeness (דְּמוּת *demuwth*). The word *tselem* means to be in the shadow of which is a Hebraic idiom for being under God's authority and covering or protection and provision. The word *demuwth* means to think like God. Not to think like a god but to have the mind of God the Father.

I believe that when God brought the animals to Adam and said, "What shall we call this Adam?" Adam said, "Well Lord, it has a long neck and spots. I think we'll call that a giraffe." I believe that God already had in His mind what it was called but wanted to see if Adam had the mind of God. And so God said, "Good, you passed that test. What about this one with white and black stripes?" Adam: "Well let me think. What would God call that? Lord, how about a Zebra?" God: "That's great Son. That is exactly what it is. That is what I called it before I created you. You pass the test." Now this illustration may not fit your theology, but the point is that you need the mind of God to lead your family. You need the mind of God to lead His Bride, the church. You need the mind of God to build healthy, functional and fruitful relationships. This is what qualifies you to be the prophet, priest and king of your house.

Pastor Keith Battles says that God looked at everything He made and said, "It is good." But there is only one thing that God looked at during creation and said, "It is not good" (Battles 2012). He looked and said man is alone. He needs a helper. Adam was content with being alone because he had relationship with God and had no concept of any other relationship. But God created a helper that the image of God may be complete in mankind, that he may reproduce himself, understand relationship, establish dominion, and complete his identity and purpose through divine unity. I am not saying that you have to be married to be complete in Christ. Christ has completed you. But it does not negate the fact that if you are called to be in a romantic relationship and pursue the covenant of marriage, then there is a divine purpose and order through which that relationship is to be built and ordered of God. Anything outside the design of God is dysfunctional. I believe dating is not biblical. For example, two dates in the Bible did not turn out well: David and Bathsheba; and Sampson and Delilah. Dating is trying out ones intimacy without the covenant commitment of marriage. It is outside the design of God.

Just as each of us are given a divine and sovereign destiny in the will of God, so each marriage covenant has a divine and sovereign purpose and destiny in the will of God. Each destiny is brought together by God to fulfill the destiny of the marriage in the Kingdom of God for His glory. Too often, we enter into relationships for selfish reasons. Most people enter into a relationship with Christ initially out of selfish motivation. They came to a point in life where they either experienced a crisis or realized they were empty.

They came to the revelation that they were sinners and could not save themselves so they needed a deliverer to get them out of the mess they were in and pay a debt they could not pay. That is probably how we all came to Christ (Pratney 1998). But at some point in the relationship, we must grow to love and honor the relationship out of a more mature love. Not just because He saved us, delivered us and redeemed us but simply because He is God and He first loved us. We must grow to a mature love that says, "God I will love you even if I have nothing, lose everything, or if you never do anything else for me beyond saving my soul."

The same must happen in our other relationships. We must remove the selfishness from the relationship. Most relationships are broken and destroyed because of selfishness. For example, a lot of men enter into the relationship, not because they are looking for God to bring them a wife, but because they are slobs and need a maid. They don't treat their wives as Christ treats the church; she's just their live in chief. They don't want a wife; they want a good electric blanket at night or they just want someone to replace their momma. Some women often don't want a man who really follows God but instead follows them. They want a man they can tell what to do. They don't want a husband; they want a handy man. They don't want a husband; they want a cute puppy. Some women want their husband to learn to hear the Spirit of God for their family but he cannot hear the Spirit of God above them being his personal Holy Spirit. These are just a few examples of the poor reasons we enter into relationships and why relationships are mostly dysfunctional and we blame everyone and everything else but never consider that we do not have a biblical view or foundation for right relationship.

Your wife or husband was intended by God to complete you, not to be used by you or to wait on your every need while you are slothful and self-serving. God gave each to one another to have relationship one with another through relationship with God, bring life to one another, and to reproduce that life through increase.

The Father gave life to man and, with woman, they were created in the same unity of relationship to produce life. As such, in the spiritual sense, we are to be life givers, encouraging, loving one another and admonishing one another to righteousness through Christ Jesus. This is the pattern of Christ as a life giver. We are to be imparters of the hope and life through Christ that dwells within us. But this principle existed long before pro-creation. It existed before the foundations of the earth. Before it was written, it was God, for God is life. It was the Law of God. Before it was written, man knew the Law of God. He was instructed to work, to know God, to seek God, to love God, to have relationship with God as well as his fellowship with man created in the image of God. He was instructed not to listen to another's voice, not to transgress the instruction of God, not to think his or any others authority was above Gods. Even with Cain and Abel, Cain knew in his heart that life was sacred and taking the life of another was to go against the will of God. Thus, from the birth of family, God gave us a blueprint of how the family should normally function designed in His image. But the blueprint was not followed and the family became dysfunctional.

The book of Proverbs provides a pattern for instruction, impartation and development of divine principle based family. In the first book of Proverbs, Solomon outlines areas of discipleship for children and parents through relational impartation of godly instruction, wisdom and discipline. In Proverbs 4:1-4, we are instructed, "Hear, my children, the instruction of a father, and give attention to know understanding; for I give you good doctrine: Do not forsake my law. When I was my father's son, tender and the only one in the sight of my mother, He also taught me, and said to me: 'Let your heart retain my words; Keep my commands, and live.'"

The Body of Christ will increase and be healthier in each generation when we start living and teaching these principles to our children. We must begin to understand that when the church grows and wins, our families grow and win. When the church is healthy, it means your families are healthier. The church team is only as healthy as the home team. If one family is broken and sick then the whole church is broken and sick. If we teach our children that church and fellowship in Christ with other likeminded believers is not really important, it's just somewhere we go on occasion, when we do not have something else more important or entertaining to do. We are teaching them that the Word of God and the authority of God in their lives is not really a high priority. We devalue the fellowship and relationship building with likeminded believers of the light and way of Christ; living together in the light, equally yoked, is not really relevant. Thus, biblical thinking, righteous living, and God pleasing lifestyle is not really important and being relationally connected to the same kind of people is of little or no significance in your life. You see, the greatest responsibility God has given you in this life is that of a parent. God has given you the task of molding and shaping the heart, mind, will, spirit and soul of another human being that He has entrusted to you. But the relationships in the home must be healthy and founded in a sincere and devoted relationship with God the Father. It has been proven that children grow up emotionally healthier in a home where there are healthy relationships between the mother and father; parents and children; and children and siblings. And to whom has God biblically given the primary responsibility in molding and shaping those relationships within the family? He has given it to the fathers. Most women who sincerely love God desire a husband who truly knows how to have godly and healthy relationship. She will love him, serve him, and be loyal and faithful if he will truly love her as Christ loved the church; if he will sacrifice and die to himself and lay his macho ego and fleshly pride on the altar before God. The Man of God must get rid of his egoism and resolve to be an altruistic leader after the example of Christ. He has to first be a servant, full of compassion and selflessness; he must be willing to serve, expecting nothing in return, not even platitudes and accolades. If you, as a father, do not know how to serve your family as Christ, then you cannot know love as Christ loved the church. Fathers have to deny the cultural ideas of whose role is what in terms of serving one another and serving the family. It does not matter who takes out the trash or mows the lawn as long as the whole family is learning that it works as a team. If something needs done, you just do it for the good of the whole family. Demonstrate your love and affection one to another as a family.

As I listened to the news one morning, they were reporting, with great enthusiasm, the newest statistics regarding the work place. They said that almost fifty percent of the workforce is now women working outside the home and the majority of those are single mothers. They boasted at the shifting of our culture to fatherless homes and successful career moms who leave the kids home alone. I said to my wife, "They are proud of that? Do they even understand the implications? That means that in a large majority of the homes in America, children are raising themselves. Families are fatherless and in so much debt that they are dismembered."

Contrary to popular opinion, and apparently the world's idea of measurable success, I see this as not a good thing. It is one thing if a woman or man wants to work and have a career but if you are a parent, you must not sacrifice that divine role at the altar of materialism and hedonism.

Imagine if you were driving along a road where a cliff was on either side. Suddenly, your car was out of control and the highway department had only placed one very solid road barrier or guard rail on one side of the road. Unfortunately, as you tried to regain control, your car hit the one rail then bounced to the other side of the road where there was no barrier or rail and off the cliff you went. Sounds tragic, I know. But would you not have desired that they had placed a strong safety barrier on both sides of the road to keep you on the road instead of going over the cliff? In the same manner, a father and mother, through the wisdom of God, are to help provide those barriers in life for their children as they grow; to be there to ensure they do not go over the cliff.

I understand that we have many single mothers. I am in no way demeaning them but instead I admire and pray for them. What I am admonishing are several things:

1.) We do not have to accept the world's glorious concept of the new norm for families.

2.) Mothers do not have to try to raise kids alone. Spiritual Fathers in the Body of Christ need to mentor and be a barrier for these children.

3.) Father's need to begin to walk in their God given responsibility.

If anything, my greatest admonishment here is for fathers to be responsible and accountable and be a barrier of truth and grace to save a generation from going over the edge of destruction. In 1 Kings 1:5-6 it says, "Now Adonijah the son of Haggith exalted himself, saying, 'I will be king.' And he prepared for himself chariots and horsemen, and fifty men to run before him. His father had never at any time displeased him by asking, 'Why have you done thus and so?'"

Let me rephrase this into language that the modern-day man can relate to. "Now Bob, Jim's son, was self-centered and self-serving. He thought he was 'King of the Hill.' He had lots of man toys and after work did his own thing. He hung out with the guys whenever he wanted. When he was growing up he had no father. Now that he is a father, he doesn't spend much time with his son. He only gets him two weekends a month and when he does have him, he pretty much lets him do whatever he wants. He does not want to upset or deal with his son's attitude if he tells him 'no'. There is no accountability or responsibility to anyone but self."

Unfortunately, this is the predominant generational pattern in today's culture. Where there is no accountability, there is no maturity. Where there is no maturity, there are no boundaries. Lawlessness and pride become the rulers that lead to destruction.

Because authority has been so abused, we have thrown it out and view it as intolerant and judgmental.

But biblical authority in righteous relationship brings true life. In the love of the Father, it keeps you from going over the cliff. As a result, righteous conviction of the Word and Spirit of God has gotten a bum rap in the church due to religious legalism and spiritual child abuse. We confuse the intent and Spirit of the Law of God with the letter of traditional ordinances. We have confused freedom with lawlessness. But lawless liberalism leads to self-destruction through humanism and antinomianism.

Any relationship worth having is worth building, investing into, and establishing boundaries to protect it. As a parent, you do not get a vacation from parenting. It is a lifelong commitment of selfless service and sacrifice. If you do it God's way, with a desire to please God, the rewards are tremendous and eternal. It is all in your attitude, perspective and seeking of godly wisdom. People say, "Kids do not come with an instruction manual." I strongly and adamantly disagree. It is called the Word of God, the Bible. But like anything else, you have to read the instructions and apply them. The right attitude and perspective helps along with consistency and the right motive behind each act as a parent. The toddler years are not terrible they are the window of opportunity to mold and shape the will of the child to accept boundaries and be content with "no". Oh, that more adults had such when they come to God the Father. The pre-teen years are an opportunity to teach responsibility, lay the foundation of identity and shape biblical thinking and healthy relationship development.

The teen years are not something to be dreaded, but seen as the opportunity to shape values, priorities, and lead them to a personal relationship with Christ. All of this depends on the environment and integrity of the home. If you are still subscribing to the old church philosophy that your family can be dysfunctional at home but the perfect Christian family at church, then the results you want from Biblical parenting will be very little.

There are many issues in the home that family problems are often tied to. There are financial issues, in-law issues, parenting issues, infidelity, and lack of trust. Then there are issues of frustration, disappointment, mistrust, abuse of authority, and lots of drama.

I have a course I teach on biblical parenting. It includes biblical instruction in many areas, such as a biblical pattern for discipline and how to call out the gifts and callings of God in your children. I am always amazed at how many people say they need this class, and sign up but never show up. Or they attend one session and I never see them again. This in itself is quite reflective of their parenting problem. The saddest thing is that those who do attend are always mothers and never fathers. I even ask, "Where is your husband?" And the answer is typically, "Sitting at home watching television." Then these very people are the first to come and want me to spend hours counseling with them about their children that are out of control.

These issues always lead to lots of drama in the home and relationships. Some families thrive on drama. If there is not some drama going on, some feel the need to create drama. When you are frustrated, disappointed, angry, or discouraged, it affects our relationship with others. We seek to find something or someone else to blame and lash out at as the target of our disparaging emotion. When in actuality, it is a reflection of the fact that something or someone, including self, was more important than our devotion to Christ. When we are hurt, some will turn to something or someone; others will withdraw from relationship; while yet others will increase their work activity. Again, it is a lack of dependence on and devotion to our relationship with Jesus Christ. Some people will pursue ungodly relationships. This points back to a lack of depth and understanding of the love of God the Father.

For many Christians, there is no real desire to place God on the throne of their hearts or allow Him to rule in their lives and relationships. Instead of giving Christ a throne in their lives, they give Him a "Loveseat" (a cushioned sofa that seats two). Because only one person

can sit on a throne but two people can sit on a "Loveseat". This way they can sit next to Christ with equal authority and still proclaim to be in love with Him. They can maintain their place in life and still give Christ a courtesy seat. Instead of having a real relationship where God defines their identity and sets the boundaries as the sovereign authority in their lives, they believe they can live how they want to live, but still have Him there to cuddle up to when they need comfort in times of trouble or when they feel the need for Him. God does not want to put on a *Snuggie* and have popcorn and a movie with you. That is not the relationship He is seeking from you. God wants to live on the throne of your life.

For many people, their relationship with family and even their church family are like a sitcom (short television drama); a little drama and a little pleasure but with limited time or commitment. We live in a culture where every day, life is like a sitcom. We have limited time and cannot pay attention except for a few minutes with commercial breaks (selfish hedonism) in between segments of our segregated lives. As a result, everything is a drama. We live from crisis to crisis. Relational chaos and dysfunction are the norm. Relationships are somewhat virtual in nature, with a touch of reality, but often at the same time on the same channel. I like to watch a cable channel called "MeTV". They have all the old sitcoms like Bonanza and GunSmoke. This is the way many people live; their whole life is always on "MeTV". They are always living in the past and having to dig up the old drama and relive it. Some of it is not even in color, its old school, but we hang onto it. They have retro-relationships. They cannot develop new or healthy relationships because they are stuck in what once was. They cannot allow God to take them into the depths of right relationship His way, because they refuse to allow God to change the channel. It is still all about them. They are stuck on "Me-TV".

Today, we have new technology called a DVR (Digital Video Recorder). If you miss it, you can always record it and come back to it to enjoy it later at your own convenience. You can even pause a live television broadcast, do your own thing, then come back and pick up right where you left off. This is exactly the perspective so many people have of relationships. They say hurtful things, do spiteful things and take the real relationship for granted. We think we can just put it on hold, then selfishly come back to it later. They hold grudges; keep record of wrongs and expect the other person to just deal with it. What is lacking is a true understanding of how love is supposed to function in and through Christ Jesus.

All of this relational dysfunction is not the relationship of the New Testament church nor is it the quality and command for which Christ gave His life.

Where there is compromise, immaturity and sin in your life, it will also be in your family, in your children, and in every relationship you attempt. Everything you do, or fail to do, is some form of investment into whom and what your family is to become.

Your relationship with God and family impacts your relationship with others. He that loves not, knows not God, for God is love. In reverse, it commands, "God is love and if you know not God, then you cannot love. You cannot know real love in your family; you cannot have a real relationship in a marriage; you cannot have healthy relationship with your children without knowing the love of God and living by the law of that love.

At the core of the atheist belief is the idea that selfishness is a virtue. It is about esteeming self above others and all else; you do nothing for anyone unless it benefits you or gives you selfish pleasure or gratification. The question begs, "How can an atheist love their children, their grandchildren, their husband or wife? How can you look them in the eyes and say you love them when you do not know love?" Love is self-denial; abasing self; self-sacrificing; putting others above self; giving of oneself unselfishly, expecting nothing in return.

The way your family views God will come from how the family functions. The measure and quality of relationship that you can extend toward others is a reflection of how you learn, view and value love and relationship in your family. Thus, how your family learns, views, and values love and relationship is dependent upon how you teach, view and value love and relationship. Therefore, you have to recognize and acknowledge where your views and values do not line up with the Word, will and ways of God. You have to purpose and commit to make the necessary biblical adjustments in your life. How you view and value right relationship is directly proportionate to your perspective and value of your relationship to God. Regardless of how you grew up or what relationships have been in your past, God can help you change both you and your relationships for the future.

According to my father, I came from four generations of dysfunctional family. My grandfathers were alcoholics. They drank rubbing alcohol, after shave, fire starter and anything that they could strain the alcohol out of. My father had learned to drink the same from his father by the time he was twelve years old. He said that grandfather told him that the only difference between a drunk and an alcoholic was that the alcoholic could more often afford better liquor but the drunk would drink anything he could get his hands on. He said grandfather would send him to the drug store to get rubbing alcohol and tell him to be sure to get the clear and not the colored because the colored stuff could kill him. Grandfather taught him how to strain aftershave through light bread and a sock. Now this is something to learn from a father at twelve years old. Today, many kids are learning about pornography and many other destructive sinful things at ages much earlier than twelve. For those who have no father, the world has become their role model or they are left to teach themselves through ungodly entertainment. They are learning from ungodly teachers and peers at school as hedonism, materialism, socialism, relativism, and liberalism have become the new school masters.

My father may not have learned how to be a good father from his father, but when my father gave his life to Christ Jesus, God taught him how to love, how to have compassion, how to lay his life down, how to surrender and sacrifice for the good of others and the glory of God. God taught him how to die to self and addictions; how to embrace the love of God; how to be a man of honor and integrity; how to show compassion and lead his family. Someone had to break the pattern.

So many today come from a long line of dysfunctional families and relationships and so many have little or no idea how to have real, right, and healthy relationships. But if you will embrace the principles of Godly relationship in your life, apply them, and allow God to lead you, He will show you how to be a godly husband, father, or wife, mother and leader in your house. God will show you how to have right relationship and how to love you family. But you have to stop the excuses and blame shifting and choose to break the pattern of destruction and dysfunction. The world does not know how to heal dysfunction because they have rejected the Healer and His healing process. Instead, they redefine dysfunction as the new normal and attack those who do not conform to their new norm.

Sadly, we have the same scenario in the Body of Christ. There has been a pattern of relational dysfunction. The church is supposed to be the pattern of righteous relationship, not ruined relationships. But we have justified it and called it everything from church hopping to church splitting. Some even dare to call it the will of God and the calling of God on their life, when in reality, they are relationally dysfunctional and the only way they can maintain and sustain any kind of relationship in the church is if they are in charge and in front. It comes down to this: we do not know how to have right relationship in the Body of Christ. Prophet Kevin Leal put it this way, "God is trying to build a family that functions like an Army" (Leal 2012). In other words, it sticks together; it defends one another; it depends on one another; it walks in unity and under the authority of God in command; it embraces, raises, builds, trains, and sends to bring increase to God's kingdom.

It is time for the church to take authority over the destruction and dysfunction that surrounds us, and bring life back to family. When will we make the choice to break the pattern of relational dysfunction? Someone has to be willing to take a stand and say, "You know I went to a church for years and no one knew my name. Instead of being offended, I am going to change the pattern and get out of my seat and show the love of the Father to as many as I can." You might be one who has said, "Well, I have been in this church and that church and all I got was wounded, hurt, and offended." Then change it. Don't take your relational church dysfunction into another church. Let the relational dysfunction stop with you. Don't be part of the pattern of relational dysfunction that has carried on in the church from generation to generation and don't sugar coat it with a super spooky spiritual so-called Holy Ghost blow out. It is amazing how spiritual we can be in the Body of Christ but remain completely and utterly relationally dysfunctional. We can lead big ministries but carry offenses all the way through it. God is not pleased. We walk out of meetings saying, "Wow, that was an awesome service. Did you see how many people fell on the floor? The ushers couldn't even keep up because they were falling so fast. And the revelation was so deep and the Spirit of God so thick." But we continue to go home content with all the relational dysfunction that remains. What have we accomplished? Nothing! If we do not have love, we are nothing.

I continue to admonish my congregation, "Though we may be few, let us be a consecrated few." I saw a slogan once on the side of truck that said, "Large enough to serve but small enough to care." We need each other. It is the will of God that you are relationally healed and that your family is healed. It is God's will that you be the best father, mother, husband or wife, not that you know how to be but that He knows how to be. It is the will of God that you know how to have right relationship with Him, with your family and with others.

The antidote to depression is gratitude. The antidote to dysfunction is sacrifice, confession and repentance; restoration, restitution, and reconciliation through the love of the Father.

There is an art to building families. God will teach us the skills to be master builders and master artists. Jeremy Fox once said, "The difference between a novice and a master is the master makes it look easy as if it comes natural" (Fox 2013). The reason is because he has listened to and followed instruction of another master. It applies to master martial artists, master painters, master carpenters, and master electricians. Whatever the field, the master has acquired the right knowledge and skill sets; underwent the sacrifice of apprenticeship; been proven and affirmed to be a master. The master makes it look easy because they have been trained and know what to do, when to do it, and how to do it right. God wants to make you a master family builder but you have to follow the Master. God wants you to know how to build a strong and healthy marriage rather than just have one and try to suffer through it and survive. God does not want to live in a marriage that you hope makes it. He wants you to let Him make the marriage.

My wife told me on our fourteenth wedding anniversary, "Well, I can believe now that our marriage will make it from here on out." I was taken back and asked why she would say such a thing. She said, "My parents divorced after fourteen years and I thought that if we made it past that fourteen year mark, we could make it." Little did I know, that during those fourteen years, my wife was living in fear for our marriage. So many, even in the church, are living in similar relational fear and God wants to heal you today.

As a martial arts instructor, one of my students at testing approached my instructor who is considered a master fifth degree black belt. He asked the student, "Who is your instructor?" The little boy replied, "Master Marvin!" Later that day my instructor came to me with a grin on his face and said, "So you are a Master now?" I laughed and said, "No, he meant Pastor Marvin not Master Marvin."

God has blessed me with many talents. I am an artist, a drummer, guitarist, pianist, singer, song writer, author, preacher, soldier, and martial artist among other things. But none of that is worth anything if I am not a master of relationships. The greatest skill I desire is to know how to build healthy relationships. My life and all that I accomplish is worth nothing if I have not first mastered the art of relationship with my God, my wife, my children and my brothers and sisters in Christ.

God wants to teach you to be a master husband and father; a master mother and wife. God wants to make you a master of relationship in your family, your workplace, your church or wherever He leads you.

Worldview of Relationship

The Bride of Christ is supposed to be the example of perfect relationship because she has the perfect mate whose name is Jesus and He has redeemed His bride from all dysfunctional relationship that was ultimately the result of sin and iniquity. Therefore, as Christians, we are called to be a different people than the unbeliever. As Christians, we are to live differently, act differently, and think differently. Your entire worldview is supposed to have been transformed to the mind of Christ. According to Dr. Paul Doherty, a worldview is made up of presuppositions or assumptions that may be true, partially true, or even entirely false which are held consciously or subconsciously, consistently or inconsistently about the basic makeup of the world. It defines who you are, where you come from, why you are here and where all things are headed. A person's worldview shapes their ethics, their values, perceptions and interpretations, thus defining their behavior or conduct as a result of the choices they make. If a person is making bad choices, it is a result of a bad worldview. Bad choices always lead to bad consequences and never good outcomes. Somewhere between the foundation of a person's worldview and the choices and outcomes of one's life, are the values and the things that define who they are. This is why it is so important that as a Christian, you seek and embrace the mind of Christ, making Him both Savior and Lord (the sovereign authority) and embrace all of Him through relationship. In that relationship, through His Word, we *da'ath* (discover God). As we continually discover God, our desire (*'ahabah*) continually increases to *yada'* (to know intimately) our God.

Again, all relationship has to begin with a sincere desire from both people in the relationship. Where there is not mutual and mature desire, there is never depth of relationship. The desire leads to a pursuit and discovery of the persons in the relationship. Through that discovery and pursuit, a covenant is made and intimacy that bears the fruit of life is the reward. In the case of our relationship with Christ, the fruit of life are the fruits of righteousness, peace and joy. What are the fruits of righteousness? First, they are made evident in your life through the choices you make; how you live your life; how you treat other people; how you handle relationships; how you manage and steward things in your life; and the way you either live for God, making Him Lord, or live for yourself. But too often, in the Body of Christ, we want to skip *da'ath* and *'ahabah* and try to go straight to *yada'* with God. When you skip divine desire and divine discovery and try to go straight to intimacy, it perverts the relationship. As a result, you end up trying to skip covenant because your flesh does not like the commitment and cost of self-sacrifice. You later find that the desire was not a holy desire in the will of the Father, it was a selfish desire by the lust of the flesh. Many Christians pervert the relationship with God in the same manner because they do not have a Holy desire for God. They seek Him for what he can do for them in their assumed faith. As a result, they do not take the time or effort to truly discover Him through His word. Thus, they assume to know Him based on what another voice said and pervert the relationship. All this is the result of having an unbiblical worldview.

How is it that in the Body of Christ, so many professing Christians can be so far from a biblical worldview? How is it in the Body of Christ, we have justified so many things that are contrary to the Word of God, yet proclaim to have such profound and in-depth revelation? So much of the church condones sexual perversion and immorality in the pews as well as the pulpits. Silence is acceptance or approval.

I have people come to me wanting a prophetic word from the Lord about which new home they should purchase or which color of new car they should purchase. I so want to tell them, "God really does not care which color car you buy. People are dying and going to Hell every minute and you think God is concerning Himself with indecision about the color of your new automobile? You are not even faithful to pay your tithe in obedience to God's Word, but you think He is concerned with which new vacation home you want to buy?" Yet, when it comes down to what to do with their money, who to date or marry, and where to go to church or when to leave a church, suddenly, they can hear the voice of God clearly and with great accuracy; suddenly, they are prophetically experienced and in need of no help or godly counsel. How can this be? Because their worldview is wrong, it is not biblical.

When Jesus said in Matthew 12:34, "For out of the abundance of the heart the mouth speaks," and Proverbs 4:23 tells us, "Keep your heart with all diligence, for out of it spring the issues of life," he was referring to the fact that your words and your actions are the result of your thoughts, and your thoughts are the result of your heart and values which have shaped your worldview. Therefore, your worldview has a significant impact on the health and well-being, or the dysfunction of your ability to have and maintain right relationships for a lifetime.

In this life, if a man tells me with his lips that he hates and despises me, I have learned to believe him and trust what he says. Often we excuse things we let come out of our mouth in anger, then come back and want to say we did not really mean it. Yes you did. What you really mean is that you did not mean for it to come out and be heard. Maybe the words came in the moment of anger but the anger, envy, and jealousy is in your heart and was the driving force behind the words. The anger is the result of a flesh and will that are not crucified and surrendered to the perfect will of God and a mind that still does not have the complete worldview of Christ as the sovereign authority.

As a result of this, we take the same worldview in which the secular world deals with relationships and we bring that into the church and our church relationships. As Christians, we are called to pursue and desire perfect relationships and relationship development that is supremely different from that of the rest of the world. The Apostle Paul dealt with this, and many other issues of worldview, as pagans were being converted and coming into the family of God. They brought with them all of their issues, their baggage, social and immoral junk. Paul had to teach them things like, "We do not worship Yahweh the way you worship the pagan goddesses. When we speak with a heavenly tongue, it is not a demonic chant. It is the power of the Holy Spirit of God. We operate of a different Spirit."

So as we in the church build relationship, we do so out of a different Spirit than the rest of the world. Pastor Harry Thomas said, "Instead of us living among evil doers in this world, it should be that we have evil doers living among the righteous in this world" (Thomas 2013). The problem is our presuppositions, and thus the reason we have negated our responsibility to define the culture we live in. Instead, we have allowed wickedness to define it and bring the depravity of the world around us into our homes and churches. There may be evil doers in my work place but they are among the righteous as long as I am there because I choose daily to think, act, speak, think, and live differently by God's standard of righteousness. Even among them, I live by a different Spirit, a different Law, a different set of values, a different worldview. It should be evident to all evil doers. If the righteousness of Christ is not evident in your life even among evil doers, then you are just like Lot and living among evil doers. The problem many have with God is not intellectual but moral. It's not that they struggle with the lack of reasoning or logical evidence of His existence, but the hypocrisy of those who say He exists. As well, it is the reality that if He does exist, they must resolve that there is a moral absolute standard, transcendent accountability, and eternal responsibility. The problem with those who once believed but no longer do, is that they were in many cases disappointed when God said no, or they were relationally wounded and carry an offense against God and all who profess to represent Him. Do your circumstances in this life dictate your love and obedience to Him? Will your personal disappointments in your present determine your eternal relationship with God and others?

You have to have God's worldview of relationship. When you do, it changes the way you enter into relationships, as well as develop and maintain relationships. It changes why and who you have relationship with. It changes the way you value relationships. All of your relational issues flow out of the heart of a true and sincere relationship with Jesus Christ because your worldview has changed. It does no good to have a "What Would Jesus Do" bracelet while you are cursing your neighbor. There is nothing gained by a fancy Bible cover with a nice little handle while you are cheating at work and cutting down your boss. You must have God's perspective of His relationship to you and your relationship to Him and to others. To know God is to be intimate with God. If it is important for you to have great relationships with people at work because you need that job, that money, and that promotion; yet, your relationships with your wife and kids is dysfunctional and you don't even care anymore. If you would rather spend more time at work than at home with your family, then your worldview and relational value system is all a mess.

Therefore, a Biblical worldview of relationship to God and family affects your relationship with others. If your relationship with God is broken, then your relationship at home is probably not healthy. If relationships at home are not healthy, then relationships at church and at work are probably not well either or are non-existent. The health of relationships works from the top down with God being at the top. You can have seemingly good professional relationships in the workplace and still have dysfunctional relationship at home and with God. But if you have a healthy relationship with God, He will show you how to have healthy relationships across the board.

I told our congregation once, "I value your relationships. They are treasures to me from God. When someone leaves out of offense instead of divine destiny, it tears my heart and soul because I value each and every relationship." It is so unfortunate that some people leave a church that they may have even been in for years because the pastor has not called them in a day or two. Relationships in the Body of Christ have to grow to the place that they are built on more than emotional insecurities but on a mature love through Christ Jesus. We need to develop securities in relationship by understanding and trusting the value of relationship. This is not to say that fellowship is not important to relationship development. Fellowship, *Chaber* חָבַר in the Hebrew, means joining together in unity or to make an ally, and is the glue of relational security. You cannot build relationship with God or His church without fellowship. Fellowship is part of learning to *da'ath* God and his people. Many want to have relationship with the head of the church (Christ) but think they do not need the Body of Christ (the church).

Many relationships start out with insecurities. Insecurity is often the biggest problem in most relationships. However, the antidote to insecurity is maturity in Christ. When Christ returns, He is not returning for a childish or adolescent Bride, but a mature Bride.

Have you ever had a dream that was so vivid and so real that when it woke you up, you were actually doing whatever it was you were doing in the dream, such as crying? One night I had a dream like this. Later my wife said that she was concerned because I was kicking, swinging and crying out in reality while asleep. In the dream, I was a mighty and strong white horse and riding me with reins in hand was Christ. It is interesting to note that the definition of reins is "the seat of feelings or passions." Christ was riding with the reins in one hand and a sword in the other. We were charging with all of our might and coming directly at us at full speed was a large black horse full of evil, darkness, and death. The closer we got, the more intense the dream felt. Suddenly, we clashed into one another and the horse turned into a demon and I began to wrestle with him but it was like wrestling with a shadow. It was gnashing its teeth and growling. Then I cried out and demanded, "Who are you and what do you want?" And he said, "One by one I will take them out with the unsurrendered issues of their lives." I cried out to God, "What is happening God?" God replied, "There is a battle for My church." Friends, the most effective way the enemy destroys the church is through our relationships because the majority of the church does not have a Biblical worldview of relationship. They do not have God's mind on the matter. As a result, many are wounded in the church and the families in the Body of Christ are just as broken as the rest of the world. In the church, we use terms like "spiritual parents", "brothers and sisters in Christ", and "covenant". However, we have misused, abused, and perverted their principles. Prophet Kevin Leal states, "God's answer to misuse and abuse is not disuse, but correct use through the integrity of ministry."

It is only in right relationship that there is authority to speak into the life of one another. Without true Biblical authority in our lives, through right relationship, we live void of responsibility, accountability or boundaries in our relationships. I cannot be a true pastor to those whom I do not have right relationship with. I cannot speak or impart into their lives. Without relationship, they will not receive direction, instruction or correction. We must develop relationships where we are not easily offended and trust is not violated. In a right and true Biblical relationship, every opportunity is an opportunity to grow into the mature or full stature of the likeness and unity of Jesus Christ.

In John 17:19, we find the first worldview of relationship and its values. Jesus states, ""And for their sakes I sanctify Myself, that they also may be sanctified by the truth." The word *sanctify* (*qadash* קָדַשׁ) means to purify, set aside, keep sacred, consecrate or separate from profane things. Two things that often destroy relationships in our life are profanity and vanity. I am not referring to curse words, although vile things that come out of the mouth are as destructive according to the Apostle James, but I am referring to anything ungodly in our lives that God considers profane or unholy. Anything that stands between us and an intimate relationship with God is profane, vain, and perverts the relationship. These things, in our hearts and minds, lead us into things like gossip, tale bearing, offense or defensive attitudes towards one another.

Christ calls us to turn from such things and separate ourselves from them that we may be sanctified in truth. Jesus goes on to say, "'I do not pray for these alone, but also for those who will believe in Me through their word; that they all may be one, as You, Father, are in Me, and I in You; that they also may be one in Us, that the world may believe that You sent Me. And the glory which You gave Me I have given them, that they may be one just as We are one: I in them, and You in Me; that they may be made perfect in one, and that the world may know that You have sent Me, and have loved them as You have loved Me." If Christ is not talking about relationship then what else is He talking about? He is talking about our relationship with the Father through Him and our relationship with one another in unity through Him. He is talking about our hearts and minds being as one with He and the Father. This is the same *echad* אֶחָד as in Genesis 2:24, "Therefore a man shall leave his father and mother and be joined to his wife, and they shall become one flesh." In essence, they think alike and act alike; they have the same values, ethics, or worldview. When Scripture says in 2 Corinthians 6:14, "Do not be unequally yoked together with unbelievers," it is not talking about racial segregation, like some foolish doctrines have proposed, it is talking about being equally yoked in your mind, spirit, soul, and your relationship with God. When it makes reference to light and darkness, it is talking about righteousness and unrighteousness; that which is holy or unholy; believers and unbelievers. The use of the *Kal vahomer* rule (The principle that applies in a lesser case applies in a heavier case) need be applied.

In John 17:22, Jesus says, "And the glory you have given me I have given them." The Word of God declares that there are two things that God is jealous for. The jealously of God is not anthropomorphic. God is not jealous and envious as you and I, for our own selfish fleshly gain. God is jealous for His own glory and for that which is rightfully His through covenant. Now, if Jesus says he has given us the same glory that the Father gave to Him, what is He talking about? The word here for glory means excellence, abundance, splendor and honor (*kabowd* כָּבוֹד) as when Moses asked God in Exodus 33:18, "Please, show me your glory." And God's reply in verse 19 was, "I will make all of My *goodness* pass before you." In other words, Moses asked for God's glory and God said I will reveal to you the very best of My nature, My goodness, My kindness, My grace and mercy. Therefore, Jesus is asking for the Father to reveal and pour out upon us that same glory, goodness, nature of God in grace and mercy that we might become one with Him and the Son. He is saying, "Father, I have shown them the way to the perfection of heart and right relationship that is found in you." Through Christ, God has shown you the way to unity and harmony in perfect relationship one with another. It is important to have a Hebraic understanding of the word *perfect* here. In the Hebrew, it is *tamiym* תָּמִים which means to have complete and unimpaired integrity in accord with truth, as said of Noah in Genesis 6:9,

"Noah was a just man, perfect in his generations. Noah walked with God." The phrase "walked with God" is a Hebraic idiomatic phrase meaning Noah had relationship with God as did Adam and Enoch (Genesis 5:24).

How many relationships in the Body of Christ can you account for in your own life, where you have been wounded because of the lack of integrity in relationship? One is far too many. I had a boss one time, Colonel Phil Roser, who said, "There is no such thing as 98% integrity" (Roser 2005). He was so right. You either have integrity or you do not. If you take truth and taint it with a lie, it is no longer truth. It's like drinking Kool-Aid but say you're drinking water. Not really the same to your body. According to the Word of God, even if your integrity is 100%, your righteousness is as filthy rags without your life surrendered to redeeming power of Jesus Christ. It is the integrity of God that we must cling to and live our lives by. There are so many of these godly principles of relationship I wish I had learned and embraced in my younger years. But it is never too late to start right now. My friend COL Robert Smothers used to say, "Think it and it will happen." He was right. The way you think affects what manifest in your life.

In John 17:24, Jesus says, "Father, I desire that they also whom You gave Me may be with Me where I am, that they may behold My glory which You have given Me; for You loved Me before the foundation of the world." The word desire here again is *'ahabah* (longing for, to will to resolve and to delight in). In verse 25 He says, "O righteous Father! The world has not known you, but I have known you; and these have known that you sent me. And I have declared to them Your name, and will declare it, that the love with which You loved Me may be in them, and I in them" The world, nothing in the world, and no one who lives by the world's ways can know the Father as Christ knew (*yada'*) the Father. Here, Jesus is presenting God's worldview of relationship. To God, relationship is holy, sacred, eternal and priority. "Two things are eternal: the Word of God and the souls of men" (Doherty 1998). God does not have to worry about His Word because it is eternal, unshakable, and unchangeable but he chose to make the souls of men a priority. The man or woman who has relationship with God makes these two things their highest priority in this life. From Genesis to Revelations, the Bible is about relationship. It is about a Holy and personable God who desired and pursued a relationship with a people. Dr. Doug Wheeler states, "It is about a wedding, a marriage, an eternal covenant." Everything in the Bible points to relationship between God and man, man and his family, and man to his neighbor. When God enters into a relationship, He makes more than a half-hearted commitment, He makes an eternal covenant. God is not a god of short term relationships. When God enters into a relationship, He has eternity in mind. God does not date people and try out a relationship like we do in our culture today. We have speed dating, Facebook dating, email dating, and even text dating. There are people today who say they are in a relationship but the only communication or interface they have with the other person is through the internet or a text. This is not a relationship. We bring the same mentality into our relationship with God, "Lord I just want a quick relationship with you for a little bit on Sunday." We want to speed date God. If the pastor preaches more than 30 minutes, that is way too long of a date. We want a 30 minute get a goose bump, sing a song, mini-sermon and then hit the door and feel like we have a relationship with the God of eternity. God does not want to speed date you nor does He want a short term relationship.

Through the years, generations had in the back of their minds that if they get married and it does not work out, they can always divorce. Now people just live together and if it does not work, they just move out. There is not even a sense of remorse, not only for the broken relationship, but for the sin of fornication which violates and breaks God's heart. I am not talking about people outside the church; I am talking about people probably sitting right in your congregation. If you think you can have a right relationship with God while you willfully and blatantly live in sin and contradiction to his Word, then you do not know God very well. You might think you do, but you do not. When God enters into a relationship, it is eternal and covenantal. God wants a monogamous, personal, intimate relationship built with trust, truth, and integrity in it.

God's worldview of family relationship as well is covenantal unity. In the family where God is the focus and Father, we find our identity. Our identity has less to do with us and what we do, but more to do with the relationships we choose to have as a part of our lives, to include our relationship with Christ. This is why, when we lose someone from our life, either through death or broken relationship, we go through an identity crisis. This is why all relationships, the core of our identity and hope, must be found in and flow from Christ alone. Many young people are so eager to leave the home to go find themselves, only to discover that everything they were looking for relationally was found right there in the godly home. But, like the prodigal, when they return there is grace and forgiveness. No relationship can stand without forgiveness and repentance. In Genesis 1:1 it says, "In the beginning God..." In the Hebraic text, this passage begins with an enlarged *bet* (בְּרֵאשִׁית, בָּרָא אֱלֹהִים) which is the first letter of the Hebrew Aleph-Bet. By enlarging this letter it emphasized the importance of the symbolism of the Hebrew letter, which is that of a house. We know that a home is where a family lives. The family is made up of a covenant relationship between a father and mother; they bear the fruit of life in the image of God and begat children. The Hebraic idiom in this enlarged house is that God, from the very beginning of creation, had in mind a family in which He would begat sons and daughters, you and I. However, because of sin, we went outside the home and embraced a self-identity outside of the relationship with God. The Father sent His Son to redeem us through repentance and forgiveness that we might be restored to eternal relationship.

In John 15:8 we find God's worldview of relationship to others. First let me say, when I talk about relationship with others, I am referring to other believers. You cannot have Biblical relationship with unbelievers. You might work with, communicate with them, show them kindness and the love of the Father. Hopefully your life demonstrates the gospel of Christ to them and you share your hope of Christ with them. But you will not have *fellowship, konania, or chabar* with them in a *yada'* level of relationship. How can you have such relationship and fellowship with someone who does not share the same highest priority in your life, which is a relationship and a life that pleases God the Father? Understand that all religions are not equal. All faiths do not lead to the same god, no more than all roads lead to Texas. So, what is my responsibility of relationship to others? To your fellow believer, it is to share in the love of the Father with each other; to the unbeliever, it is to share the love of the Father with them in hope that they may be saved, without compromising the integrity of the Gospel.

Again, John 15:8, "By this My Father is glorified..." by what is the Father glorified? Remember, earlier we read where Jesus said, "And the glory you have given me I have given them..." And we said that when Adam knew his wife Eve she bore fruit; that fruit was the fruit of life and it too was created in the image of God. You see, God is glorified when your life bears the fruit of righteousness. In the fruit of righteousness through right relationship is the fruit of life. When you have Christ centered and Christ driven relationships in your life, the fruit of Christ is evident in all of your life and it impacts the life of others around you. The whole world can see that you are different and Christ lives in you. So Jesus goes on to say in John 15:8, "...that you bear much fruit; so you will be my disciples. As the Father loved Me, I also have loved you; abide in my love."

So how do you honor Christ relationally as He has commanded here? You have to die to self daily and in every circumstance or situation. You have to relinquish the excuses, justifications, and evidence of your offenses. Self has to be nailed to the cross with Christ; buried and never dug up again. Every time self tries to reach up and come out of the grave, you have to keep self under your feet. Some of us want to say we buried self but we keep a Bible in one hand and a shovel in the other so we can dig self man back up from time to time.

If we knew how to truly keep God's commandments in love, then we would surly know how to have and maintain right relationships, even with our enemies. When we understand that it is not about the other person honoring us but it is about us honoring God, then we can love the husband who is a jerk; the wife who is a nag; or the co-worker who just gets on our last nerve. When you start truly honoring God, it might just allow the Holy Spirit to change others through the love of Christ they see evident in you. They may suddenly want to have right relationship with you because God has restored desire in their hearts for reconciliation. Then when both of you are honoring God with a sacred, pure, and holy relationship, it becomes that perfect relationship that only comes through the love of Christ Jesus. But it all starts with, "If you will keep His commandments just as He kept the Father's commandments by abiding in His love."

In John 15:11, Jesus goes on to speak of the rewards of obeying His commandments regarding healthy relationships, "These things I have spoken to you, that My joy may remain in you, and that your joy may be full." The word "full" in the Hebrew is *male'* מָלֵא meaning in abundance, satisfied, accomplished, complete as in Micah 3:8, "But truly I am full of power by the Spirit of the LORD, and of justice and might…"

When the joy of Christ is full in me, then self-sacrifice is not a struggle, it is a natural part of who I am. Self-denial becomes part of my nature. When this happens in relationships, even those that once seemed difficult are no longer a struggle but joy can be found even in them. The joy of the relationship is not dictated by someone else, but by the covenant you have made with God. You may not be in a covenant with your co-workers or your boss, but you are in a covenant with God in which you reciprocate His love to Him by loving others as He has loved you. John 15:12-14, "This is my commandment, that you love one another as I have loved you. Greater love has no one than this, than to lay down one's life for his friends. You are my friends if you do whatever I command you." This is what defines your worldview of relationship and what defines your joy. Therefore, God's worldview of relationship is selfless, sacrificial and unconditional. But it is a commandment. Our flesh does not like commandments. However, commandments reveal what is in our hearts and where we are in our maturity in Christ. Commandments demand introspection and a response of accountability and responsibility for what we have chosen to be, say, or do.

I Corinthians 13:1-3 emphasizes this point, "Though I speak with the tongues of men and of angels, but have not love, I have become sounding brass or a clanging cymbal. And though I have [the gift of] prophecy, and understand all mysteries and all knowledge, and though I have all faith, so that I could remove mountains, but have not love, I am nothing. And though I bestow all my goods to feed [the poor], and though I give my body to be burned, but have not love, it profits me nothing." You might have a wonderful ministry or even be a pastor of a thriving congregation; you might operate in the prophetic with great accuracy and have profound words of knowledge; you might even have tons of Scripture memorized word for word; you might have scholarly degrees and endless revelations, but if you cannot love your neighbor, your family members, or others, then you are absolutely nothing (*shamad* שָׁמַד; nought; annihilated; destroyed; laid to waste; Deuteronomy 28:63). Without love, bugs and worms have greater significance. Some Christians even take on a martyrdom mentality in the work place to excuse their lack of Christ-like love. It is really the same as any other paranoid and victim mentality; they just have a spiritual name for it. They call it "persecution". They say they are being persecuted for their faith when in reality, they are just religious jerks that are annoying and obnoxious in the office. But they have convinced themselves they are a martyr when the problem is that they have not love. I am not saying that there are not legitimate and outright attacks on Christianity in our culture today. I'm just clarifying what is not. Sometimes in the church we blame the devil, others, and even God for our own irresponsibility, laziness, apathy, and self-abortion of destiny.

If you look at the rest of 1 Corinthians 13, you will find foundational building blocks that are used to build healthy relationships, "Love suffers long and is kind; love does not envy; love does not parade itself, is not puffed up; does not behave rudely, nor does it seek its own. It is not provoked, thinks no evil; does not rejoice in iniquity, but rejoices in the truth; bears all things, believes all things, hopes all things, endures all things. Love never fails." These building blocks are like the toy Legos building blocks that you stick together to build all kinds of things that you can imagine. Patience, Endurance, Kindness---all are fruits of the Holy Spirit. They are evidence in your life of the presence of the Holy Spirit and the transformation of your nature by the love of Christ. They are your new character and personality attributes when you became a new creature in Christ (2 Corinthians 5:17, "Therefore, if anyone is in Christ, he is a new creation; old things have passed away; behold, all things have become new."). I cannot count how many times I have gotten up in the night and stepped bare foot on one of my boys Legos that was left on the floor. It is painful. In this same passage, we find Legos that will destroy relationship and hurt the image of Christ in you when they are connected to the relationship. They include envy, pride, jealousy, arrogance, rudeness, iniquity, malice, boasting, and other such things alike that are contrary to the nature and Spirit of Christ.

I encourage you to highlight, underline and even double underline some of these as measuring tools to your relationship building skills. Have you ever gotten a greeting card where someone had underlined certain words for emphasis to express their sincerity? Then, they realized that they had gotten carried away and underlined every word so they go back and double underline certain words for double emphasis! We always joked with my mother for doing this. But I believe in this passage of Scripture, 1 Corinthians 13, these attributes of relationship need to be underlined and some even double underlined.

Love does not demand its own way. Demanding one's own way is a destructive force in relationships. Another term for this is a "controlling spirit" which is evidence of immaturity and childishness. 1 Corinthians 13:11 states, "When I was a child, I spoke as a child; I understood as a child; I thought as a child; but when I became a man, I put away childish things." I know men and women in their thirties, forties, and even older who still think childish, act childish and speak childishly when it comes to relationship issues. They never learned conflict resolution, to show affection, or be considerate of others because they are too self-centered, prideful, paranoid and narcissistic, refusing to allow God to reveal it and transform their heart by accepting responsibility, accountability and forgiveness. I love them and Christ loves them but they will never grow into the fullness of their sovereign purpose and identity or find joy in their relationships. They will always see only the negative, never the positives, in any relationship.

Verse 11 states, "He understood and thought like a child…" This means he reasoned like a child. It refers to how a person perceives, discerns, and has or has not wisdom. It refers to how one thinks of others, themselves; one's judgment and interest. It is like children in school who can say the harshest things because a child by nature always has self in its best interest at the expense of others. To *reason* means to take into consideration; to take into account; to weigh responses and courses of action; and how you make decisions. Many have never grown in these past the toddler or adolescent phases of spiritual, emotional, and mental development. The Apostle Paul states, "But when I became a man, I put away these childish ways." In other words, he grew up into right relationship.

Love is not irritable; it is not resentful and rejoices not in wrong doing, but instead rejoices in truth. Like the Legos, when you step on them in the darkness, they hurt. But when in the light, you properly connect them together with your kids and relationship building is the picture you have in mind, then you can not only build some really cool stuff but you can enjoy and build healthy relationship in sincere love. You can then call out the gifts and callings in others. If you have the right pieces in the right place, you can even develop something that functions in the Kingdom of God and brings Him glory and honor and bears the fruit of increase in Abba's house.

Love bears all things; love believes in the identity, destiny, and hope of Christ in others. Love never ends; love never fails. This brings us back to the eternality of righteous Biblical relationship from God's perspective.

In 1 Corinthians 13:12 the Apostle states, "For now we see in a mirror, dimly, but then face to face. Now I know in part, but then I shall know just as I also am known. And now abide faith, hope, love, these three; but the greatest of these is love." This term "face-to-face" is the same term used first in Genesis 1:2, "And the Spirit of God was hovering over the face of the waters." According to Dr. Doug Wheeler in his book

Betrothed, the word for *face* here is *paniym* פָּנִים meaning the presence and person before and behind; toward; in front of; on the surface and before time. It is used again in Genesis 32:30 when Jacob encounters God and says, "For I have seen God face to face, and my life is preserved." And again in Exodus 33:11, "So the Lord spoke to Moses face to face, as a man speaks to his friend." Now Scripture tells us that the Hebrews believed that no man could see God and live such as with Manoah in Judges 13:22, so how did these see God face-to-face? What did it mean? When the Spirit of God brooded over the face of the waters it meant that God's presence was not just on the surface but was beneath the waters, above the waters, and on every side of the waters. In other words, all of creation was consumed by the presence of God. With Moses, the Hebraic picture is not simply two people having a conversation face-to-face (*paniym-al-paniym*) with a comfortable personal space in between. Instead, God and Moses were so close it was like a passionate kiss (Wheeler 2012). I can imagine Moses so engulfed in God's presence that he could feel the breath of God so thick that he could hardly breathe and was panting and gasping for air.

Here in 1 Corinthians 13:12, the Apostle says, "…but now face-to-face (*paniym-al-paniym*)," referring to truth of which the attributes of right relationship flow out of for intimate relationship with God. When you have a face-to-face intimate and passionate relationship with God, it changes the way you think, the way you act, and what you desire. You no longer think like a child, reason like a child, speak to others like a child, respond like a child, make choices like a child or deal with relationship like a child. But through this relationship with God, you grow into maturity that pleases God. The Apostle continues in verse 12, "Now I *know* in part, but then I shall *know* just as I also am *known.*" Here again is that *'ahabah, da'ath, and yada'*. Though I discover God in part, as I seek Him and long for Him, I can be fully intimate with Him. When you grow in Christ you shall understand and desire, discover, and have intimate relationship in the holiness of God with Him, your family and others. God can be only as intimate with you as you are willing to be intimate with Him.

When I was in the Army, they used a concept to teach soldiers how to aim a weapon at a target and the principles of good marksmanship. The first thing the soldier has to learn is how to establish and consistently maintain a good sight picture. The same applies to your relationships. A godly perspective must be maintained of relationship. You have to perceive people and relationships the way God perceives them. God perceives every person as an eternal soul that He desires to have covenant relationship with. Each soul is His goal. God views relationship as eternal and covenantal as well. You

must have the same perspective when it comes to relationship with your spouse, children, and even your brothers and sisters in Christ. The key to having a godly sight picture of relationship is to allow the Word and Spirit of God to establish consistent stability and maturity in your life; to allow the Word of God to be cultivated in your heart and mind. That which is cultivated in the heart will manifest in the life. If you cultivate righteousness, peace, and the Word of truth, then you will reap the fruit of it in your life. If you cultivate bitterness, resentment, anger, and unforgiveness, then you will reap the fruit of such. John 1 says that all things exist by the Word of God. As such, the Word of God holds all things together that they may continue to exist. So it is in your life. If all creation is held in order and all life exists because of the Word of God, then if your life is in chaos, disorder, and is falling apart, it may be because the Word of God is not being cultivated to the point of bearing its fruit in your life.

Now, in marksmanship, every time you fire the weapon, it recoils and you lose your sight picture. A good marksman develops consistency of his sight picture and is able to quickly get himself and his weapon back in the right position, regain composure and be ready to fire again. Relationships are this way. Often, things do not go as you expect them to because there are other wills, personalities, and much more involved. Sometimes you seek to develop healthy relationship and it recoils or backfires on you. The key is learning not to let these situations set you back in your relationship with God. If your relationship with God is solid and consistent, then you do not lose your sight picture. You are able to quickly adjust your emotions and thoughts back on the will and way of the Lord.

There are four key elements involved in the development of a godly sight picture regarding right relationships.

First, there is the target. For the believer in Christ, the target is right relationship in the will and way of God. Many people are content to have good relationships but the goal of God is to have godly relationships. If a person is simply looking for a husband or wife, then they have their sights set too short. Because God wants more than just a good marriage relationship, He wants a godly, life producing, Kingdom purposed covenant relationship that is built in 'echad. In the Hebrew, the word 'echad means unity but if you understand the deeper concept in Hebraic thought, it is not merely unity as in being in agreement. It is to be fused as one in spirit and soul. This is what God meant when He said, "A man shall leave his father and mother and cleave (*dabaq* דָּבַק cling to; stay with; pursue closely) unto his wife." Or when Christ said, "Father make them one as You and I are one." So, set your sight on the target of godly relationships, not just good ones.

If the target is godly relationships, why would we settle for anything less? For starters, no good marksman uses a target that is full of holes. If you start with a target full of holes then you will not know if you hit the target or not. God can heal the holes in your perspective of relationship and your past relational dysfunction. However, you must develop and maintain the godly character to keep the target clean and clear of holes representing broken and dysfunctional relationship patterns.

When I was in the Army, there were times I would go to the range to qualify. We would put up our new targets then get in our positions and fire. When we would go down range to look at the targets, I would notice that I may have had only ten rounds but there are fifteen holes in my target. There was only one explanation; the person next to me was shooting at my target instead of theirs. Herein lies another principle; keep your eyes on your own target. Stay out of other people's business and focus on what God is trying to do in your life. Quit looking at what is going on in other people's life and getting distracted. Keep your focus on what God is trying to do in you. It may be a test of your heart. I have found that God does not test my heart once in a while, or once a week, or even every other day or daily. God test our hearts every moment.

You may not be hitting someone else's target but you may not be hitting your own as well. Some people fire ten rounds and go down and find only one or two holes in their target and wonder where the other rounds went. The problem is that they are not aiming at what we call "Center Mass." They are shooting far left, far right, too high or too low. You have to bring your relational sight picture in line with, or center mass of, the will of God. Like the clay on a potter's wheel, if it is not in the center when it starts spinning, it will begin to take on its own shape and form. It has to be in the center of the wheel. So you have to ensure you stay in the center of the "will" of God and your relational sight picture center mass on God's goals and not your own. You must maintain the authority of God in your life. You will only walk in the level of the authority of God relative to that which you are willing to follow and submit to. Your success will be relative to your level of accountability you are willing to be under in Christ. Keep in mind, that the effort you are willing to put forth in anything (to include relationships) is reflective of the value you have placed on that which you desire. How much do you value your relationship with God and others? Do your investment efforts reflect that value?

Contrary to what you may perceive from your past relational experiences, godly relationship is not a moving target. But when you keep following your own perspective of relationship, building it eventually costs you. It may cost you your soul, your peace, your family and possibly even your future. At some point, you have to recognize that something must change in you. It could be that your sight picture or worldview of relationship is not the same as God's.

The next elements in the sight picture are the front and rear sights. Like the target of godly relationship, the front sight moves up and down. The front sight in this illustration is the Word of God. It is the same yesterday, today and forever. If you will apply the Word of God in your life, it will always be on target. However, the Word of God may be either up or down in your life. If there is too little then you will miss the mark. Or if you have a head full of Scriptural intellect and not maturity to rightly divide the Word of God, then you are still missing the mark. You have to have the balance of intimacy where you are on target in your relationship with God. The rear sight can be adjusted as well. It can be moved either left or right. If it is too far left or right, you will miss the target. The same applies to relationships. If the horizontal relationships in your life such as with family, church members, co-workers and others are out of alignment, it is probably because your vertical relationship with God is out of alignment. Either there is sin in your life or heart and you are not in intimate relationship with Him or you have become so religious, spiritual, judgmental, condemning, and self-righteous that you are not in intimate relationship with Him through His covenant. As a result, no one can stand to be around you; you think it is because you are standing for Jesus; and you think the problem is with everyone else. I am amazed at how people can have a pattern in their life and never see it. They have had five or more jobs; gone through four broken relationships; and joined six different churches; changed their cell phone number and email accounts three times all in the past year and yet still will have a justifiable reason for the inconsistencies in their life and it is always someone else's fault. They cannot see that the only thing consistent in their life is inconsistency or instability. The only common denominator in everything from their church membership to broken relationships is them. If you get the vertical relationship with God right, the horizontal relationships will follow.

The final element in having a godly worldview or sight picture of relationship is the eyes. Your eyes have to see things through God's vision. You might have a good eye or bad eye but if you will see through the eyes of the Father, you can see your future, relationships and all involved, through His heart. Dr. Ron Moseley states, in the Hebrew, the term "good eye or bad eye" was a Hebraic idiom that meant if one had a bad eye he was greedy, selfish, self-centered and un-giving. If they had a good eye, they were selfless, generous, benevolent, and preferring of others above themselves or altruistic. If you are missing the target of godly relationship, you might need to check your eyes. You might be aiming at the target but shooting with your bad eye instead of your good one. Or maybe, you are shooting with both eyes closed and just hoping this relationship will work out or be the one. You might need to open your eyes; see what you are shooting at; get your sights set on God's goal of right relationship, and allow the Word of God to establish consistency in your life so that relationships stop backfiring on you. You may keep thinking, "This one", or "That person is the one for my life" but it doesn't work out so you wait a while and try it again. Or, you keep hoping this time things will work out and be different in the relationship, only to discover that things did not get better but worse. Why? Because there are inconsistencies between your life and the Word of God.

There are some things that tend to blur our vision and sight picture in relationships such as not allowing the Holy Spirit to deal with past relational baggage. When you get on a flight, you check in your baggage and do not worry about it again. You entrust it to the airline and they assume responsibility for it. However, that which you continue to carry on the flight you are responsible for. If you lose it, you cannot hold the airline people responsible for it. The  Holy Spirit is the same way in that he is only responsible for that which you relinquish into His authority. It may be time for you to check in your relational baggage and let it go. Many people continue to carry things in their lives that they were never meant or designed by God to carry. These things continue to blur godly vision of godly relationships such as abandonment, rejection, abuse, infidelity or past mistakes. Maybe you came from a broken and dysfunctional family. Maybe all you have experienced is dysfunction in the church and you carry wounds from disappointed expectations of what were supposed to be godly and biblical relationships. I have discovered that every church title or denomination has its share of baggage. When people ask me, "What is your denomination?" I just say, "I just love Jesus and fear God." What are you? Are you a prophet, pastor, evangelist, apostle, teacher? I simply reply, "I am an obedient servant and son." I don't want all the baggage that the church has associated with its titles and labels. I just want to honor and be intimate with God Almighty. That is not to say that I do not know who I am and what my sovereign call, purpose and identity is in Christ. I am simply stressing the fact that we need to put more emphasis on seeking and pleasing God than pleasing men and their collection of ministerial baggage.

In Matthew 11:28-30 Jesus says, "Come to me, all who labor and are heavy laden, and I will give you rest. Take my yoke upon you, and learn from me, for I am gentle and lowly in heart, and you will find rest for your souls. For my yoke is easy, and my burden is light." And 1 Peter 5:7 states, "...cast all your anxieties on him, because he cares for you."

Next, a lack of trust and insecurities blur or distort your perspective of relationships. You come into the relationship seeing through the lens of your insecurities and thus have preconceived fears, paradigms, presuppositions, offenses, and hurts refusing to allow God to heal or deal with the dysfunctions of your life. Many do this with relationships, not only in their personal lives, but also in their church life. They move from church to church, never able to commit or stay and develop healthy relationships because they come into a new church and bring the same dysfunction. I have found that when someone wants to leave the church they will always find a justifiable offense in which to leave. Often, the problem is that they never really wanted a deeper relationship with God in the first place. They are not looking to grow or help the Body of Christ grow. Every church has its baggage and dysfunction. Some hide their dirty laundry better than others. However, when Christ returns, He is coming for a functional family, not a dysfunctional one; thus, the motivation for this book is to prepare the Bride of Christ. When you allow the Holy Spirit to deal with your insecurities, He will tear down the walls and help you to trust again in the God of relationship and the relationships God places in your life (Proverbs 3:1-8; Matthew 18:21-35).

Finally, selfishness blurs your sight picture of healthy relationships God's way. Envy, jealousy, ambition, hedonistic desires, false or unrealistic expectations, and anger blur godly relational vision and will destroy relationships. (Regardless of how you justify your wrath and anger, unless it is righteous indignation against sin, first and foremost in your own heart, sinful anger destroys not only relationships but lives.)

Proverbs 27:4 says, "Wrath is cruel, anger is overwhelming, but who can stand before jealousy?" In Genesis 3:1 we see where the *nachash* נָחָשׁ beguiled mankind and hindered the relationship between God and man. In Hebrew, *nachash* is the word for serpent. It is defined as to be beguiled, deceived, or manipulated. At its root, it is defined as learning from one's own experience. This is where the Hebraic concept of iniquity, or the propensity to rebel against God's will and do one's own will, is derived.

In Genesis 4:3-10, Cain brings his offering to God and God rejects it because of the iniquity of his heart. We often assume it was because Cain withheld a portion or brought the worst of his crop. However, it just as well could have been that Cain brought abundance and the best but with pride and haughtiness against his brother. Maybe he was trying to show himself better than his brother and God rejected his heart. Kind of like those Jesus spoke of who ring the bell when they bring their offering ensuring everyone hears how much they had contributed.

In either case, God tells Cain in verse 6, "Why are you angry? And why has your countenance fallen? If you do well, will you not be accepted? And if you do not do well, sin lies at the door. And its desire is for you, but you should rule over it." God warned Cain that sin was at the doorway of his heart, that it was about to destroy his relationship with God, his entire family, and future. But in the very next verse, it says that Cain not only ignores what God said, but premeditates and commits the murder of his brother.

We do it in the church. We ignore what the Word of God says. We premeditate our sin as we convince ourselves that we are not really gossiping but our motives are pure. We tell ourselves we sincerely intended to pray for our brother's issues. We tell ourselves that are not in sin; we are truly seeking God's will in finding out if this person we are dating is truly the one as we commit fornication with them. Then when confronted with our sin we get an attitude. Prophet Kevin States, "All sin will manifest in an attitude."

Why would you choose to marry, enter into a lifetime commitment and plan for your future, with someone who does not know how to have right relationship? As well, God wants a Bride who knows how to have right relationship. God wants you to know the full joy of relationship God's way; relationships built on the love of God.

In every relationship, sin is always at the door. It is for us to take the authority of Christ and rule over it. In 2 Corinthians 10:4-6, it says, "For the weapons of our warfare are not carnal but mighty in God for pulling down strongholds, casting down arguments and every high thing that exalts itself against the knowledge of God, bringing every thought into captivity to the obedience of Christ, and being ready to punish all disobedience when your obedience is fulfilled." I hear Christians quote James 4:7 half way. They say, "Resist the devil and he will flee from you." But they fail to remember the key to resisting is found in the first part of this verse, "Therefore submit to God." Half obedience is not obedience at all.

God wants to have right relationship with you; a relationship that you do not dread or despise but a deep and intimate relationship. Some people have just resolved that they will keep walls up and give up on right relationships. But God wants to change your worldview of relationship and help you see the joy in having relationship as God intended.

God is not looking for your affiliation to Him but the affirmation of your affection for Him.

Redefining Intimacy

The God of Abraham, Isaac, and Jacob is a covenantal god, a generational god, and a god of relationship. In true Christianity we do not serve a religion, but we serve a Holy God. It is from that covenant relationship, all other relationships must flow. God first loved you. He did not choose to love you because of anything you were, could do, or could be. He chose to love you because He is love. Some say to their self, "I will start serving God once I get my life all together." That is like saying, "Once I save myself I will serve the Savior." Therein lies the problem that must be sacrificed on the altar, self. You can never save yourself; that is why you need a savior. Christ is that Savior. We so often have the same obstacle in relationships. The thing that destroys any relationship is selfishness.

Notice that Jesus said in Mark 12:29-34, "The first of all the commandments is: 'Hear, O Israel, the Lord our God, the Lord is one. And you shall love the Lord your God with all your heart, with all your soul, with all your mind, and with all your strength.' This is the first commandment. And the second, like it, is this: 'You shall love your neighbor as yourself.' There is no other commandment greater than these." Notice that Jesus adds an important phrase in between the two that we often overlook. "And the second, like it, is…" You cannot separate the first from the second. You cannot say you love God and not love your neighbor, even if they are your ex-wife or ex-husband. You still have to love them with the love of the Father. In 1John 4:20, it says, "If someone says, 'I love God,' and hates his brother, he is a liar; for he who does not love his brother whom he has seen, how can he love God whom he has not seen?" And 1John 4:7 states, "Beloved, let us love one another, for love is of God; and everyone who loves is born of God and knows God." If you cannot love your brother or sister in Christ, then you do not know God and do not know love and cannot say you love God. I know our flesh does not like this at all. But had we figured this out, we might not have burned so many relational bridges in our past.

We have already stated that if your relationships with others are unhealthy, it is a good sign that your relationship with God is not healthy. You might say, "Yeah, but what about the will and responsibility of the other person or persons involved in the dysfunctional relationship?" That is between them and God. You are responsible for your integrity and motives of your heart before God. If you will stop the blame shifting and just focus on your heart and perspective and embrace God's, then the love of the Father can bring the reconciliation He desires, when He desires. Prophet Nick Stevens says, "You can either be right or be reconciled." You have to be sure that you are on God's side and are willing to reconcile when and how God sees fit. It is like Joseph and his brothers. Joseph was certain he had forgiven his brothers until God placed them once again in front of him and the resentment rose again in his heart. The dream of his brothers bowing before him was less about his rise to power and more about his humility, brokenness and willingness to forgive. The dream was not about a future but about forgiveness. You will never fulfill your destiny in Christ or walk in your full identity in Christ without forgiveness. You cannot have right relationships until you learn to live a lifestyle of forgiveness as Christ did. Forgiveness, like love, is a choice. You have to choose to forgive as did Christ and Stephen. As they stoned Stephen for preaching the gospel, he cried out in Acts 7:60, "Lord, do not charge them with this sin." If I learn to live a lifestyle of forgiveness, then I cannot be easily offended, because when you do something to offend me, I have already learned to forgive you. It is called spiritual maturity. Christ had already learned to take on your sin and forgive you unto death before He ever faced the cross and felt the nails being driven into His hands and feet. How could He and Stephen have such strength over their flesh? It was because they had learned to be intimate with God; they had learned the art of Godly intimacy; they had learned God's definition of intimacy.

In our culture, when the word "intimacy" is heard, the first thing in our minds is something physical or some sense of perversion. The Devil and the enmity of the hearts of men have so perverted the idea of intimacy. Throughout Scripture, we find where God spent much time confronting, setting boundaries, and dealing with the perversion of intimacy. Even after Noah; after God has rid the earth of all the wickedness and perversion, the son of Noah goes into his father's chamber and commits acts of perversion. In Genesis 9:22 it sates, "And Ham, the father of Canaan, saw the nakedness of his father, and told his two brothers outside." If you look in Leviticus 18, you find a pattern of this Hebraic idiom, "to uncover another's nakedness." In the Law God addressed every manner of sexual perversion. Why? Because men were doing it. What is the point? The point is that God has continually and continues to this day to deal with the perversion of intimacy in the hearts of man. Man continues to try to excuse it, redefine it, and further pervert it. Even in the church, true intimacy in family has been perverted and the divorce rate in the church is as high, or higher, than the rest of the world. Even intimacy with God has been perverted and replaced by religion, personal agendas, hedonism, doctrines of men and devils. As well, much of the church has come to accept, justify or overlook all kinds of sexual immorality and we wonder why God is not truly present in our churches. Prophet Kevin Leal said, "God will not dwell in or work through an unclean vessel" (Leal 2012). Ephesians 5:3 states, "But fornication and all uncleanness or covetousness, let it not even be named among you, as is fitting for saints..." Anytime intimacy is perverted, or redefined outside the scope of God's boundaries, it destroys relationship with God and others. I have counseled with so many couples who are struggling in their relationship and always find a pattern that if they have been sexually active with each other or others (outside of the boundaries of Biblical covenant marriage), it was a defining moment of relational dysfunction. Kevin Leal states, "Often, things don't go wrong, they start wrong." Only when they have first repented of sexual immorality in the relationship can God begin to redefine the relationship according to His will and reconciliation take place.

In God's view of intimacy, it is an act of eternal commitment. It is an act of selfless devotion. It is sacred and holy. Therefore, it must be guarded and kept pure, free from vanity and perversion. It is given freely in divine consecrated covenant. It is monogamous and a treasure.

Intimacy in any shape or form outside of the boundaries of relationship as defined by God is perversion. It defiles that which God has set in order.

So, even masturbation, by definition, is pleasing self in context of sexual gratification that is outside the design of God, which was preserved for a man and a woman in covenant relationship of marriage.

My wife and I were in the process of adopting a child. We had to take mandatory classes in the process. We sat in a class room full of Christians, even some pastors, youth pastors, and worship leaders. Some people were there to qualify for adoption and others for foster parenting. The subject of masturbation came up in the context of discovering a foster child in the act. I listened as so many of these Christians responded by saying they would just tell the child it was natural, it was okay, just clean yourself up and all kinds of craziness. I told my wife, "What are these people being taught in their churches?" We wonder why families are so messed up, homosexuality and other perversions are so rampant, and the innocence of our children is being stolen at earlier and earlier ages? We ask ourselves why the divine institution of marriage is being so attacked and destroyed. The church itself has redefined intimacy. All forms of perversion come from the same tree be it homosexuality, pedophilia, pornography, fornication, masturbation, lust or adultery. Jesus said it all starts from the same seed of iniquity in the heart and minds of men in their enmity against God. So much of the church does not even have a clue of how God defines intimacy, purity and holiness. When I talk to a 25 or 30 year old man or woman and use the word "fornication" and they have no clue what that word even is, yet they truly believe they have an intimate relationship with God even though they are living in complete sin and rebellion.

There is a difference between sex and intimacy. God made both. There can be a physical act of sex yet be void of intimacy. Even in a marriage, there can be the act of sex but no intimacy. What destroys the intimacy is when one or both seek only to please self and seek only selfishly to take and not give unselfishly to please the other. There can be perversion even in a monogamous marriage. If the wife comes to the husband and says, "If you will give me some extra shopping money, I will give you sex tonight." You have just perverted and prostituted the intimacy of the marriage. You defiled that which God made holy and sacred in the covenant. In 1 Corinthians 7:3-5 it says, "Let the husband render to his wife the affection due her, and likewise also the wife to her husband. The wife does not have authority over her own body, but the husband does. And likewise the husband does not have authority over his own body, but the wife does. Do not deprive one another except with consent for a time that you may give yourselves to fasting and prayer; and come together again so that Satan does not tempt you because of your lack of self-control." Is the Apostle saying that the body of the wife belongs to the husband and that of the husband to the wife? No! They both belong to God; the marriage belongs to God; the intimacy belongs to God! It is a statement regarding the defining of intimacy by God in that it must be kept "selfless".

True intimacy only comes when the relationship is defined by the holiness of God's boundaries for right relationship. The Hedonistic "free love" movement pushed sexuality to the extreme of perversion, but never lead to a pure undefiled intimacy. Sexuality often stems for a search for true intimacy that only comes through a right relationship with God. God put a desire for intimacy within you; First and foremost that you might know pure and intimate relationship with him. Anything less is simply a giving away of your soul in exchange for a moment of pleasure that still leaves you empty (Wilson 2009). That's why Paul wrote in 2 Timothy 2:22, "Flee also youthful lusts; but pursue righteousness, faith, love, peace with those who call on the Lord out of a pure heart." Jesus defined true intimacy as this, "Love the Lord your God with all of your heart, soul, mind and strength." Here, Paul lists key foundational elements of building healthy relationships God's way. They are starting points for developing intimacy with God and restoring relationship with family and others. It is amazing that here, as well as many other places, the Scriptures lay out for us how to have healthy functional relationships, yet so many continue to live in and struggle with dysfunction in their church and family. If only we would begin to apply these principles to our lives. First he says, flee youthful lusts. This not only applies to sexual immorality but also youthful appetites, ignorance, pride, impulsiveness, childishness and the like of immaturity and rebellion. He is not talking about age but attitude. I have discovered that some people have simply a goldfish level of relationship capacity. By this I mean, the level of responsibility and accountability they are prepared and mature enough to handle in a relationship is having a goldfish that does not talk back or require anything of them; all they have to do is feed it a few flakes every now and then and change the water from time to time. Some people only grow to puppy level. They are willing to pick up the poo and still love the puppy. God wants more than goldfish or puppy level love out of His people.

Second, Paul says for us to follow, chase after, or live by righteousness, faith, love, and peace and with them call out to God with a pure heart. Paul is addressing the principles that govern the intent and motives of your heart in and for relationship. In this one passage, he is giving the keys to having and maintaining right relationship. He is talking about your attitude, reconciliation, conflict resolution, and every kind of issue that you could imagine concerning relationships. Notice that nowhere in this passage does he say to follow your own opinion, your heart, your feelings or emotions. All of these attributes that Paul says to follow after must flow out of a right and intimate relationship with Jesus Christ. If God's relationship with you depended on His emotional opinion from day to day or circumstance to circumstance, with as many of us who are inconsistent, we would all be in big trouble. God would have already de-friended you on His Facebook page. God intended for us to have face-to-face relationship with one another as with Him. Godly intimacy is built on Godly characteristics. It is built on spending time with one another through joys as well as hardships. True relationship does not turn to childish and immature anger in the face of accountability. It resorts back to the steadfast heart and love of those in the relationship who have proven faithful and true to the best interest of God and everyone in the relationship. It does not end a relationship through a text or email, but does due diligence to search the heart and flesh, humble one's self before God and seek the road of reconciliation. True intimacy is this, "Love the Lord your God with all your heart, soul, mind and strength. And love your neighbor as yourself." Many Christians know this part but there are a few very important parts we often skip over. First, "Hear, the Lord is one God (*echad*). In other words, He is a God of unity. Second, He says, "The second commandment is like unto the first." In essence, you cannot separate the two. They are one and the same. You cannot love God and not love your neighbor. He affirms this in conclusion in Matthew 22:39 and Matthew 12:29-30, "On these two commandments depend all the Law and the Prophets; There is no greater commandment than these." When you have built a relationship with God and build other relationships on the principles that the Apostle Paul sets forth, then you can truly begin to learn how God views intimacy. True intimacy is not merely physical, but an issue of the heart. If your relationship with God is solely based on a feeling as to what you perceive as His presence or love for you, then you are missing out on true intimacy with God. You will then take this same perspective of intimacy into other relationships and will only sense security and worth in the relationship as long as you feel it. The love of God is more than a feeling. We all want to feel that we are loved, hear that we are loved, and be shown that we are loved. God has provided all three. But the security of your relationship with God does not come from even these, although God has said it, sent it, and shown it. His love for you is not based on a feeling, but a choice. Your greatest security in this love is this: knowing that He is God and He does not change or lie. He first loved you and wants an extreme intimate relationship with you and desires for you to reciprocate that same desire. God does not want a fling with you but a lifetime monogamous relationship.

From the beginning, God's desire has been to build a family. As such, he has demonstrated through the life of Christ how a father commits all of himself to the service of the family. Many fathers today believe that the extent of their service to their family is to go to work, go play and do their thing, then come home, flop down on the couch, turn on the television and bark orders. That is not the end of the responsibility to serve your family. Pastor Len Ballenger says, "We need more fathers not Pharaohs." I believe this to be true both in the home and the church. In Genesis 2:24, God described it this way, "Therefore a man shall leave his father and mother and be joined to his wife, and they shall become one flesh." There is a point, when building biblical intimacy, where two people grow together beyond just a familiarity of one another. For example, I have a deeper relationship with men in the church who have labored for years in the Kingdom of God at my side than I have with the guy down at the convenient store. The level of relationships do not compare because we have loved together, laughed together, hurt together, and labored together. Our relationships have withstood many tests in life that reveal or prove the depth and sincerity of relationship: 1.) Time; 2.) Adversity; 3.) Promotion; and 4.) Loyalty. True godly relationships are built on: 1.) Love that covers sin but holds one accountable and admonishes true growth in Christ; 2.) Covenant; trust; a friend that sticks closer than a brother; and 3.) Commitment that changes not, regardless (Johnny Barham 1986). There is a difference between relationships and acquaintances or those you become familiar with. For example, you can develop a familiarity with God through the Word but not have relationship. You may know what you know of God based on what your parents or pastor told you. You and someone may write each other letters for years and become familiar but never really know them in terms of relationship. Familiarity makes one think that they are given special liberties in the relationship. If there is not 100% concern for the partner and no selfish motives in the relationship, then it is a dangerous relationship and one will go into the relationship with ulterior motives in mind. These same misconceptions (false sense of relational depth or familiarity) of relationship can often happen in families where a couple thinks they have a deep relationship with their spouse but instead it is just familiarity; or parents grow to just have an acquaintance with their kids and no real depth of relationship. Then one day, they wake up from their business, in a crisis with their child, and discover they did not really know their child because they had never really been involved in their life.

Again, in Genesis 2:24, Moses defined covenant relationship with three key words "leaving" and "Cleaving" and "one". To leave in Hebrew is עוב *'azab*, to leave behind, abandon or to forsake. In order to have true intimacy with your spouse, you have to enter into a covenant, forsaking all others and preferring them even above yourself. This sounds like a wedding vow because that is exactly what it is. All of Scripture is about God desiring an intimate relationship with His people and entering into an eternal covenant. Any attempt or form of intimacy outside of the divine vows of covenant in God leads to a perversion of intimacy. This Hebraic concept of leaving what was, to embrace what is and shall be, means you cannot be in a covenant relationship with your spouse, yet hold onto old relational baggage, photos of your ex or old lovers. You have to bring all of you into the relationship not just parts. You have to leave all of your old relational baggage behind or it will weigh down the momentum of relational development. You cannot maintain a relationship with old flings while trying to have an intimate relationship with your spouse. You cannot have true and pure intimacy with your spouse while you have others on your mind or images of others. This is a form of adultery that perverts the intimacy. You have to leave all else behind, and cleave (רבק *dabaq*) your spouse. In Hebrew, this means to closely pursue, be eternally deeply attracted to, to join together with, to

115

remain with steadfastly, and to stick together. This is why romantic relationship outside the covenant of marriage struggles or fails because it is missing this element of divine defined intimacy. They can never truly become one flesh (אהד '*echad* – meaning alike, one will, united, in unison, eternally bound together and inseparable).

There are some couples who felt an attraction when they first met, so they pursued one another. They did everything possible to be where the other one was and seek to be noticed and opportunities to interact one with another. Then after years of marriage, they can't stand one another. They avoid one another and get on one another's nerves. It seems every little thing the other one does is just annoying, and there is no pleasure in the relationship to be found. They may even have sex occasionally, but it is just to please their selfish fleshly craving but there is no real relationship because they have lost the Godly concept of *dabaq* or to cleave as God desires to cleave to you and you to Him.

John 17:11, "I am no longer in the world, but they are, and I am coming to You. Holy Father, keep them in Your name (YHVH-Creator, Father, Eternal Covenant God), which You have given Me, that they may be one, even as We are one." (Also, John 17:20-22) Here Jesus speaks of Him and the Father being in '*echad* (one heart, one mind, one Spirit, one will, perfect unity). As well, He asks the Father to bring each of us in His church into the same '*echad*; to be in unison, willfully and richly bound together in the love and Spirit of Christ as we are one bride married to Him.

What Christ envisioned was what we would today better term as a network of committed relationships. Today our relational networks are all in virtual time and space. Our relational network development is more through a mouse and a monitor than it is with face-to-face friendship and fellowship. Christ's intent was that this network of committed relationships would be the goal of all of our efforts and activities as believers. But we now live in an age where convenience trumps commitment of effort to have deep and meaningful relationship one with another. We say, "Drop by my Facebook but don't drop by my house"; "Shoot me an email but don't send me junk mail"; "Text me a line but don't waste time calling"; "I'll see you on Sunday unless Sunday becomes just another day."

In Biblical Hebraic mind-sets, every action a person takes involving another reflects his character. Every interaction between men is reflective of the level of relationship between them. Every area of life, regardless of how significant or insignificant we view it, is considered by God as a step toward developing a mature, eternal, covenant relationship in the Spirit of Christ (Intrater 1989).

Let me give you a covenant example. If we made a trade of goods, the exchange of goods has a lasting spiritual importance beyond the mere exchange in the eyes of God. It demonstrates an opportune step toward determining whether we could trust each other in the future to have a continuing relationship. My honor and your honor before each other and God are at stake (Intrater 1989). There are so many opportunities in our lives from day-to-day that we either miss or do not consider as divine opportunity for covenant relationship.

As well, there is the issue of covenant potential. Many areas of our lives that we would ordinarily consider steps toward covenant relationships in Christ actually involve some level of covenant probability from a Scriptural perspective: Helping someone in need, random acts of kindness, attending a Bible study group, attending worship, giving to one another, kind words, and sharing in one another's sorrows and joys are all acts of cooperative covenant. Every time you worship, give, pray, or call upon the name of God, it is a step of covenant. Every word you speak backed by your personal integrity is a step towards covenant (Intrater 1989).

One morning I was on my way to the office. I stopped at a three way intersection. Across from me there was an elderly lady on her walker. She was trying to bump her trash cans to the street curb. I stopped at the stop sign, put the car in park and got out and offered to help her. While helping her, others approached the stop sign but were held up for a moment as I crossed the intersection and helped the lady. You could sense and see that they were irritated by the short delay due to a random act of kindness. This is often how so many of us are in the relationships of our lives with our families, church members, and others we encounter possibly by divine providence. I may not have developed an intimate relationship with this lady but I may have planted a seed of the mercies of God that enriched her intimacy with the Father.

Then there is always the issue of covenant-keeping. Too often in the Body of Christ, many terms get perverted and abused. The term "covenant" has no less been used by church leaders to manipulate for personal agendas. So many in the Body of Christ have sought to become true spiritual sons and daughters only to experience what Prophet Kevin Leal calls, "spiritual child abuse" (Leal 2012). This is just like the Devil to pervert, so as to prevent that which draws us closer to the Father and into our divine identity and destiny. Thus, from the Biblical perspective of covenant, it then becomes important to tear down walls of past relational perspectives and seek to develop lifetime relationship with those of like covenant in Christ, and to *azab* עָזַב or forsake all ungodly relationships and *chabaq* חָבַק or embrace an *echad* relationship with fellow believers, brothers, and sisters in Christ. From God's perspective, every action in life, every single syllable you utter about yourself or another in the covenant Body of Christ, may be seen as an extension of character and therefore as an act of covenant-keeping or covenant breaking. From this divine perspective, no part of our daily lives can be viewed as merely mundane. Everything we say and do with each other should be done as an expression of the love and Spirit of Christ Jesus (Intrater 1989).

Throughout Scripture we find that God is a covenantal God, generational God, eternal God, and relational God. God views everything through the eyes of eternity. God never enters into a temporary or short-term relationship. He always enters a relationship with eternity in mind. When you mess up, God does not seek to quickly terminate the relationship because He consistently has eternal covenant in mind. When you enter into relationships, what do you have in mind? Do you have the mind of God regarding the relationship? What about your church family? Can you envision lifetime relationships? Where are the days that children and their children's children grew up in the same church and the power of God was just as evident in their day as it was in the days of their fathers? We have lost godly perspective of relationship.

Our families are in the same situation. It amazes me that so many professing Christians stand and look each other in the eyes in a wedding and commit to stay with each other in the covenant of marriage "In sickness and in health until death do us part" but shortly after are filing for divorce because of offenses. So, we committed to sickness and health but not offenses unto death? You see, the problem is we did not consider that what needed to die, in order for the marriage to survive, was our own selfish flesh. We no longer enter into relationships with eternity in mind. Covenant within yourself today means that you have eternity in mind in your relationship with Christ, your family, and His Body.

Communication and Insecurities

One of the first things the enemy does when he seeks to destroy our relationships is to pervert desire for relationship with offense. Once the seed is planted, we withhold biblical relational communication. Once we allow the enemy to destroy the desire for continued or deeper relationship, the seed of mistrust is planted in us and we isolate or alienate ourselves from the relationship. That seed then grows in the fertile soil of our insecurities instead of the richness of God's Word and love. With each and every relationship destroyed or severed, a portion of our identity and destiny is distracted, delayed or destroyed.

Two of the biggest issues that cause relational dysfunction are poor or unbiblical communication and personal insecurities. Often the enemy will use the open door of our insecurities to instigate gossip, build a spirit of discontentment, and bring division. Given a platform of insecurities, the enemy will build a monument of pride and develop a victim mentality in our hearts and minds. He will play on the emotional dysfunctions of the soul.

If the filter of our heart is not that of the Word of God and selfless love of the Father, then what goes through our thought process affects our emotions, thus affecting our relational health and wellbeing. It is like a coffee filter. A coffee filter is a simple technology that in today's world of high technology we think little of. But if you think about what it is designed to do, it gives some insight into the way our souls function. My grandfather was an alcoholic. My father tells of how grandfather would take light bread or something to use as a filter and strain aftershave or Sterno fire starter through it in order to separate the alcohol so that he could drink it. Now that is desperate, but the point is that the filter separated the contents of that which was strained through it. You can place a coffee filter in the right place of a coffee maker and fill the filter full of coffee grounds and when you run water through it, you get coffee. The flavor and quality of the coffee is dependent upon the richness of the coffee and water you put in and through that filter. If you put dirt in the filter, you are going to get muddy or dirty water. So, whatever I put in the filter will determine what I get out of it. Relationships work in the same way.

God has given you a filter. For many people, the day-to-day relational filter they use is that of their emotions. They filter everything people say or do towards them through their emotions. This is most often not healthy for relationships. It is like the coffee filter, if it has holes in it or the filter is weak and not strong enough, you get grounds in your coffee. When you take a drink and get a mouth full of grounds, you want to spit it out. If you are not using the right filter for relationships, that might be the reason you always leave relationships with a bad taste in your mouth. That may be why you are so often quick to spit out relationships easily without hesitation or remorse. Your emotions are a bad filter for relational development.

Some people filter relationships through their past experiences, past relationships, or the dysfunction of their own families and assume that all relationships function that way. We filter future relational possibilities through the way people were treated in our home or what happened in another church. As a result, we begin to stereotype certain situations, circumstances and even personalities and we filter everything through that mindset. And because our filter is messed up, God is not able to bring about complete healing and restoration in our lives because we are still interpreting everything through a bad filter.

When you have a bad filter, you are going to get all kinds of nasty things in your relationships like discontentment, envy, jealousy, anger, resentment, bitterness, mistrust, division, pride, haughtiness, arrogance and offense. These spirits then come in and divide and destroy, because they know that you were created for relationship.

Another filter that the enemy loves to destroy relationships with is your imagination. This is where you begin to imagine all kinds of things to be offended or wounded about that are most often not even reality. You childishly begin to imagine the worse and all kinds of evil thoughts about others as perpetrators against you instead of letting your first thought be love. You get to the point that you are convinced that there is no good in anyone's heart; no one can be trusted; and everyone is out to get you; take advantage of you and are focused on wounding you. You fail to remember that the only good in any of us is because of the love of the Father. This happens very frequently in marriages until it becomes a self-fulfilling prophecy, often the result of the progressive dysfunction and relational degradation.

The filter God has given you is as simple a technology as that coffee filter. In fact, in most Bibles, the pages are thinner than most coffee filters but the Spirit and the truth of the Word of God is the strongest, purest, and best filter you could ever have in your life. If used properly, with the power of the Holy Spirit running through you, it will produce the finest and richest relationships you could imagine. When you use the Word of God as your filter, right perspective flows from it, right thinking, right communication, right authority, right interpretation, and right relationships flow from it and all impurities such as pride, envy, deceit, misunderstanding, miscommunication, jealousy, offense, and insecurities are filtered out. You can then drink the life that flows from the heart of Father in relationship.

Isaiah 59:2 states, "Behold, the Lord's hand is not shortened, that it cannot save, or his ear dull, that it cannot hear…" At the very first of this passage, God addresses relational communication. Then He goes on, "but your iniquities have made a separation between you and your God, and your sins have hidden his face from you so that he does not hear." Here He addresses the hindrance to relational communication and effectiveness. He begins to address the things that cause relational dysfunction.

Again, the word iniquity is that inclination to rebel against the will, word, and ways of God. It is that desire to please self and the flesh. It is derived from that same beguilement and self-deception that poisoned relationship in the Garden of Eden (the garden of relational pleasure and delight in God) known as the serpent or in the Hebrew, *nachash* נָחָשׁ found in Genesis 3:1.

God says here in Isaiah 59:2 that your iniquity and your sin relationally separate you from God. I assure you that most of the time, they are the same things that separate other relationships in your life. You see, Jesus came and died for your sins, but He also came to confront your iniquity. Many Christians continue to struggle in their walk with Christ because they do not have a living awareness of their righteousness in Christ.

Their conscience is weighted by their iniquity instead of driven by their righteousness in Christ. So instead of walking among the living that are quickened alive in Christ, they are still professing to be alive in Christ but walking around in their old grave clothes like Christian zombies. When Christ called Lazarus out of the grave, one of the first things He told them to do was get those grave clothes off of him. When Jesus rose from that tomb, he left the grave clothes behind. Ephesians 2:1-3 states, "And you were dead in the trespasses and sins in which you once walked…" Apart from the resurrecting, life giving power of Christ in your life, you were a zombie. In the Body of Christ there seems to be a lot of Christian Zombie-ism (people professing to be alive in Christ but still living in the damnation of sin and trying to pull others into their heresies of death). Romans 6:11 tells us, "So you also must consider yourselves dead to sin and alive to God in Christ Jesus." I think that sometimes in the Body of Christ we get grace confused with gravy. You see, grace is sweet and might even go well with biscuits but it is not a license to feed your fleshly appetites with lawlessness. God has the plan and the blueprints of your life. You are neither the architect nor the builder. You are that which He is building. The house does not say to the architect, "I don't like this wall there or the way that room is laid out." Nor does the house say to the builder, "I don't like the hammering of the nails." The foundation has been laid in Christ and you and I get to be co-laborers with Christ in building His Kingdom and building up others

(Standford 1982). You were created for relationship and called to the ministry of reconciliation of souls in right relationship to the Father. Many are called but few are chosen." Often the difference between being called and chosen is your willingness to submit and commit yourself to the process and preparation of answering the call. When you stop being a hearer of the Word you become a hearer of something else besides the Word of God.

One of the most important things in a relationship is good, effective, and consistent communication. Healthy relationships demand that there is a continuity of communicable connectedness. If a husband and wife are in a marriage and they never communicate one to another except when they are angry; or it is always one way communication; in either case, it is not a healthy relationship. Even if they give each other the silent treatment or communicate on a regular basis but it is always screaming and using hurtful or cutting words, or with sarcasm, it does not produce a healthy relationship because they are not truly hearing one another. They are using the wrong filter instead of the Word of God. Instead, they are using the filters of selfishness, childishness, their flesh or sinful nature that they supposedly had died to when they came to Christ. They are not communicating through the filter of righteousness in Christ. Just as our iniquities (inclination towards evil; desire of the flesh against the will of God) and our sin (disobedience to the will and ways of God) separate us from Him, so they are the predominant factor in what divides us as a people. Just as we are divided as believers, so we are divided from the totality of the Spirit of God. God is a God of unity in His will, His ways, and His Word. You cannot have healthy relationship without effective two way communication. Sin is the biggest problem in our ability to communicate and have right relationship. When we allow our sinful nature to be our relational filter, there is always a breakdown in communication because you cannot hear the truth of God in the relationship. We let our iniquity redefine His will, His ways and His word according to our own justification, thus dividing us from right relationship one with another. The unity of Christ comes through unity with Christ and there is no unity with Christ if we are not truly in Christ. Therefore, iniquity and sin inhibit our ability for God to clearly communicate His will and way to us. As well, it hinders our ability to communicate relationally with one another leaving us with communication gaps and barriers to relational development one with another. If we have pre-conceived ideas and perceptions about things around us and in our lives that are contradictory to the character and Word of God, we will refuse to hear it and continue to be blinded to truth because of our iniquity. As a result, we never grow to relational maturity in God through His Word. Often God's communication to us is skewed, misinterpreted, or completely rejected because of the way we hear through the filter of our iniquity.

If you embrace this concept and allow the Holy Spirit to begin to work His work in and through you in this area, it will transform your life and the relationships surrounding you. You will learn true effective communication, even in relational hardships, as God communicates His love to us. This could be no more demonstrated than through the history of the people of God throughout the Old Testament.

In Ezekiel 14, God cuts them off from His face, from communication with Him, because of their rebellion and iniquity against the Spirit of God. In verse 3 God says, "These men have taken idols into their hearts." What does God consider an idol? God considers an idol as anything that is exalted above God; that which takes precedent in your life demanding your affections, desires, and priorities. An idol does not have to be an object, or graven image, it can be something in your heart. You can easily make your ministry, vision, gifts and callings, or service to God an idol. You can quote the promises of God in Scripture and make them an idol of which consumes your passion instead of the God of the promises. As well, anything that demands your submission to it instead of obedience to the Spirit and Word of God is an idol. Ezekiel 14 goes on to say that they had "set the stumbling block of their iniquity before their faces." The same word is used here for "faces" as when Moses met with God face-to-face, *paniym*, meaning they had become intimate with the object of their sin and temptation. Notice that God then asked the prophet a question, "Should I allow Myself to be consulted by them?" Remember, when God asks you a question, it is not because He is lacking or in need of information (Ballenger 2012). It is for your own introspection and self-evaluation of your heart and thoughts in the light of Him. Often, when God speaks to us and asks us questions, we are so self-consumed that we want to give Him our opinion. We are so busy telling Him what we think that the only thing we can hear is our own mouth running, much less what God is trying to instill into us. God is trying to give us the answers to our life issues but we are too busy interrupting Him with our will and self-centered ways. God asked the prophet, "Should I even entertain their inquiries?" It is like the preacher to whom God reveals the Word of the Lord to directly give Godly wisdom, counsel, direction and instruction to the issues of a person's life. The preacher gets up and delivers the Word of the Lord that Sunday morning but the folks whom God intended it for and who need it the most decided to sleep in that Sunday or go do something else more entertaining. Or, they, at the very moment the Word of the Lord for their life is delivered, have to get up for the third time to go get a drink of water and hang out in the lobby and fellowship because they do not have enough attention span and maturity to sit and listen to the Word of the Lord. However, the very next day or as soon as the service is over they come to the Pastor and want to schedule private counseling regarding the very issue the Lord just addressed in their life but they were absent without leave. What the Pastor should tell them is simply, "No need for private counseling, get the CD." In like manner, God had given them the will of God but they did not follow it and now they want God's counsel. But God goes on to tell the prophet what to say to them. God states His desire for them, which is to turn their hearts to destroy their idols so that He might reconcile them unto right relationship with Himself again. God addresses His heart and motive in contrast to theirs.

Verse 7 states, "For any one of the house of Israel, or of the strangers who sojourn in Israel, who separates himself from Me, taking his idols into his heart and putting the stumbling block of his iniquity before his face, and yet comes to a prophet to consult me through him, I the Lord will answer him Myself." First let me say, I have always been amazed at how people will sit in a service and I can preach a very strong and straight forward message from the Scripture relating directly to their sin issue and yet they will, with no fear of God, come and request a prophetic Word from the Lord. I want to just say, "Are you for real? Thus saith the Lord, Stop sinning! Repent and sin no more!" But here God says, "I will answer him Myself and cut him off from Me and the midst of My people!" God is saying, "I will sever communication with those who are of the wrong spirit." Now if God is so serious about having communication or relationship with those who are not after His Spirit and instead follow the spirit of devils and contradiction against His Word, then should not you and I be as serious about our relational communications? The last person you want "de-friending" you is God.

God continues by saying, "If the prophet says nothing to the people then God will do the same to him." God says, "If the prophet will not speak to the situation, I will cut him off as well from My communication." Whenever the people of God allowed iniquity and sin to stop their ears from hearing the Word and instruction of God, the relationship suffered, and they began to believe that God had abandoned them or was nowhere to be found as they fell into idolatry. The absence of sound biblical communication from sender to receiver develops insecurities about the relationship. This is true of your relationship with God, in your families and with others. God offers them repentance, but if they refuse, He cuts them off for their own good that their hearts may be restored to right relationship with Him. So even in God's discipline there is grace. It is like parenting a child so that the child grows with the right perspective of identity, security of self-worth, and the value of relationship. There is no relationship where there is no accountability. There is no accountability where there is no authority. There is no authority where there is no discipline. And where there is no discipline, there is no maturity of relationship.

There has to be continual healthy relational communication out of a sincere motive of love to admonish one another to righteousness and intimacy with God. The antidote to bad communication is learning to communicate as God communicates. The key to communicating as God communicates is to first have an intimate relationship with Him where His communication flows through you; it is to let your first thought be love and learn to respond to any situation with honor, maturity, and by seeking the will of God. The key to bad communication is to operate out of a selfish, childish and immature motive. The more you learn to maintain good godly communication, the less relational conflict you will experience. You can learn to actually love and enjoy the relationships God places in your life instead of dreading and missing divine opportunities. I am reminded of the couple who had to go to their Pastor for marriage counseling because the wife said she felt that her husband just did not love her anymore after many years of being together. The husband said to the Pastor, "Pastor, I told her twenty years ago when we got married that I loved her and I would let her know if anything changed." It is one thing to say we love someone and assume they never forget it, but it is another thing to demonstrate it with your life, actions, attitudes, and choices. You need to demonstrate it with your maturity, stability, consistency, commitment, provision, protection and defense. Your wife, husband, and children ask no more of you than God asks of you. Therefore, if you cannot love your family, how can you say you love God? If your life demonstrates your love for Father God, then it will show in your relationship with your spouse and children, as well as your church family. In the previous illustration, both failed to communicate the love of the

Father to one another as God intends. Both of them had bad relational filters. She was operating out of insecurity and he was operating out of immature ignorance. If you do not know how to communicate your thoughts and feelings with biblical perspective instead of your own adulterated opinion, then you will either be offended or offend many. We must learn to hear how and what God communicates to us and learn to communicate with others in like manner.

The largest majority of our relational problems are the result of either our own or another's insecurities. Most of those insecurities are the result of something that was done or said to us from someone in our family. For many, it may be the result of something or someone in our family, where relationship and trust concepts were perverted or disillusioned. If a child is left alone from infancy and never shown affection, spoken to, given appropriate boundaries, or shown how to function, then that child will grow very dysfunctional.

I watched a documentary once of a young girl who was abandoned at birth and placed in an orphanage. She ran away and lived in the street among the dogs from which she found affection. Eventually, she grew to live, eat, and act like a dog. She walked on all fours like a dog and barked instead of speaking. In her mind she was a dog. She was taken by those who sincerely cared for her wellbeing and was rehabilitated. Today she is a beautiful and functional, intelligent and productive young adult lady. In the interview, she says that sometimes she remembers when she thought she was a dog and there is something inside that wants to revert but she refuses and remembers who she really is. The Apostle Paul describes a similar situation in all of our souls. There are two natures at war within us. One is the flesh nature or the sin nature that refuses to die and thrives on self-pleasure, gratification and satisfaction or rebellion against the nature of God. The other is the redeemed nature that has been reconciled to God to walk in righteousness and right relationship. The same applies to the iniquity in our relationship with others. Often, it seems so easy to revert back or default to our past relational failures, wounds, offenses, and insecurities rather than to filter communication and situations through the filter of the mind and heart of God.

There are several things that children must have growing up and we all need throughout our lives to grow secure in our God given identity and our ability to respond relationally with others in the family:

1. Proper nurturing and affection; Ps. 40:11; Ps. 103:4; Col. 3:2

2. Physical and emotional safety; Lev. 25:18; Ps. 4:8

3. Opportunity to grow through responsibility and accountability;

4. Behavioral and relational boundaries;

5. Confidence in who we are and our abilities for a positive future with purpose;

6. The ability to effectively communicate with others (Standford 1982).

All of these stem from a proper founding of development according to the Law of God. From these we can grow into relationally healthy family members living in maturity, wisdom, peace, unity, grace, forgiveness, and harmony. Through these, we will learn how to respond to and resolve conflict through the Biblical principles of reconciliation and restoration. We will learn to turn away another's wrath, be considerate and respectful of other's thoughts and feelings, and think before we speak.

Have you ever wondered why you experience heartache and sorrow when you have been in a relationship or friendship that you hoped would be a lifelong relationship but instead it fell apart and you were left heartbroken and with pain in your soul? You feel pain because you were created for eternal covenant relationship, never for broken relationship. You were created in God's image and as such, God is a God of covenantal relationship. Nowhere in Scripture do we find that God ever enters into a relationship with the anticipation or intent of it being a short lived relationship. When God enters into a relationship, He expects and intends on it being an eternal relationship of covenant. He always had and has eternity with you in mind. If you touch a hot stove, your physical design lets you know that something is wrong and harmful. You quickly feel pain and pull away. Your soul was designed the same way. When relationships are broken, something inside tells you it's not natural and you feel pain and grieve. You were never created for short term relationships. You were created in the image (*tselem*) and likeness (*demuwth*) of God for eternal relationship.

Ephesians 3:14-19 tells us, "For this reason I bow my knees before the Father, from whom every family in heaven and on earth is named, that according to the riches of his glory he may grant you to be strengthened with power through his Spirit in your inner being, so that Christ may dwell in your hearts through faith—that you, being rooted and grounded in love, may have strength to comprehend with all the saints what is the breadth and length and height and depth, and to know the love of Christ that surpasses knowledge, that you may be filled with all the fullness of God."

Your family name may be tied to a whole lot of emotional, spiritual, mental, and relational baggage. It may have been defined by the relational iniquity and perversion of your sin or the sin of others against you. But God is calling you to allow Him to redefine the family name and redefine future for your family. You see, the Barham name used to mean town drunk. My dad was an alcoholic by the time he was twelve years old. His daddy and his grandfather were alcoholics. God had reached out to each generation, but they refused to let God deal with their iniquity. My dad says that grandfather could quote Scripture even while he was drunk and great grandfather traveled in a wagon preaching revivals then would get drunk. But God reached out to my dad and he responded in complete surrender. God delivered our family from the curse of iniquity and today the Barham name has a new meaning--- "Men of God!" Alcoholism is no longer my heritage, nor is it my inheritance, but righteousness and intimate relationship with the God of all creation are mine and for my children and their children to come. God wants to do the same in your life but you must get the roots of old relational thinking and responses out of your soul (mind, will, and emotions) and let the roots of right relationship through Christ Jesus work in you and grow connected to the true vine through intimate relationship. In his book *Covenant Relationships*, Keith Intrater states, "Our relationship with God and our trusting relationships with other believers give us a certain rooting, groundedness and security in who we are. When we are secure in our identity, we can act out of obedience to the Spirit. If we are insecure, our actions come from an energy that is soulish or psychological in origin. Only when we are secure in who we are as a product of our relationships, will our actions be born out of faith, love and leading of the Holy Spirit" (Intrater 1989).

If the Body of Christ would learn to operate in these principles, then the next time your pastor says something from the pulpit that rubs you the wrong way, either because you don't agree or you misunderstood something, the first thought in your mind is not to take off looking for another church but to honor God by asking yourself, "Do I know his heart?" Maybe I should go to him and run my offense through the filter of love and the consistency of the Word of God he has preached in the past and the integrity of how he and his family live their lives. What has his motive been in the past? Has it always been to help my family and to help me grow in Christ? Maybe we need to do a filter check. If the Body of Christ would operate in these principles, then maybe the next time someone comes to you and wants to drop a little lying, deceiving gossip in your ear about a leader in the fellowship, you can make sure you have a good filter over your ears. When they say to you, "Did you know this about that person?" you respond with, "I'm sorry; I did not understand what you said because I have this filter, this big thick Bible up over my ear. You see, I was covering my ear with the Word of God so as to filter out anything displeasing to God." How about when the Devil is lying to you; trying to tell you that no one at that church really loves you or cares about you. Will you recognize that Satan is playing on your fears and insecurities? Will you quickly begin to filter it through the love of the Father that has made you clean? When you start having that self-talk about how you are of no value; no one wants you; you're a failure; and you are reminded of your past relational dysfunctions, you simply put that filter of the Word of God before your face and remember His redeeming grace. You need that filter that says you are His; you are a son or daughter of the King of Kings; you are seated with Him in heavenly places; He is for you and not against you. You need to bring every thought into captivity unto the obedience of Christ and cast down every vain imagination that exalts itself against the knowledge of God.

Too many people in the Body of Christ are not only living spiritually in the shadows of the valley but they are living in a spiritual swamp. God wants to lift you up to the mountain. When God wanted to speak to the Israelites, they told Moses that they did not want to hear the voice of God because of their iniquity. So they said, "Moses, you go up the mountain and hear God for us. You go be our filter from the voice of the Lord." God does not want a middle man; He wants to speak directly and intimately into your life, into your soul and spirit; into every situation; into every circumstance; and into every relationship. The only filter He wants you to listen through is His love for you and the truth of His Word about you.

A lot of the Body of Christ does not live by Scripture but by commentary. As well, people do not live by what they know relationally but what they assume in relationships. This effects their communication and perceptions that ultimately defines their responses. In Scripture, the principle is to let your first thought be love. But you cannot do that if you do not know what love is. This is why you must allow the Word of God and love of the Father to define love instead of you defining love through your own experiences and emotions. The question we need to ask ourselves is, "What defines our dialogue?" Does the love of Christ through the Holy Spirit always define your dialogue? As we mature in Christ, our approach to dialogue should shift from selfish to altruistic. The process may start with "Why don't you just move that out of my way? (Questioning)" then progress to "Move that or I'll move it for you. (Demanding)" to "Can you please move that? (Requesting)" and finally, "Where can we move this to a better spot? (Teaming)." Your dialogue with God is often reflected in your dialogue with others (Jones, 2002). If we fail to mature in our dialogue with one another and with God, we will continue to have relational dysfunction. As a result of relational dysfunction, our identities may remain stuck. Many people's identity is frozen by ungodly dialogue with self, others, and the Devil or spirits of darkness.

In Matthew 13 Jesus give s parable of seeds of the Word of God sown into the hearts of men. In verse 19 Jesus explains that the seeds never took root because they lacked understanding. The Word of God is powerful and life transforming. It redefines you and your relationships. But biblical illiteracy leads to moral depravity and enmity against Truth (Jesus Christ – the way the truth, the life).

Offenses and Forgiveness

In historical Judeo culture, the idiom of taking on ones yoke referred to being linked together in a covenant partnership (Moseley 2000). In the Body of Christ today, it seems as if it has taken on quite another meaning. Among Christians today, it seems as if to take upon another's yoke means to take up an offense with or against them. In Jesus' day, the term was most often used by Rabbi's to mean for one to take up the yoke of Torah, or to allow the will and rule of God's Law to govern your life. In doing so, you become an active partner in the Kingdom of God, fulfilling His promises (Moseley 2000). Thus, when Jesus says in Matthew 11:30, "For My yoke is easy and My burden is light." He was talking about surrender to the Law or the will and way of the Father. This would make sense as the context of the entire passage is about repentance, forgiveness, and the grace of God.

With this concept in mind, I am amazed at how Christians today can be so spiritual yet harbor un-forgiveness with the most pious self-justification. For one to profess to be a child of the King, stand in the midst of the King's presence in a church service and proclaim their love and adoration of Him, yet at the same time, give a dagger of a look across the sanctuary at their neighbor for whom they harbor an offense.

One of Satan's most deceptive and insidious kinds of bait to divide and conquer the church is something every Christian has encountered - offense. Actually, offense itself is not deadly - if it stays in the trap. What is destructive and deadly is how we respond or react to the bait. If we pick it up, consume it and feed on it in our hearts, then we have become offended. If it is something that you hang onto and can quickly recall in defense or under pressure, then it is an offense. Offended people produce much fruit, more so than most other Christians in the church. They produce fruit such as hurt, anger, outrage, jealousy, envy, strife, resentment, bitterness, hatred, judgment, critical conversation, condemnation, gossip and division instead of vision. Some of the consequences of picking up an offense are insults, attacks, slanders, wounding, separation, broken relationships, betrayal, and backsliding. It leads to misconceptions such as "everyone is in a click that I'm not part of"; "well they're just jealous"; or "they just don't like us, we're not their kind". Whenever you begin to use the words "them" or "those" people, you have an offense. Offense is not sin in another's heart but your own. Yet, it is amazing how it can come out of our own mouths and we not hear it (Bevere 2004).

No one has been more offended than God. Isaiah 53:3, 5, "He is despised and rejected of men; a man of sorrows, and acquainted with grief: and we hid as it were our faces from him; he was despised, and we esteemed him not. He [was] wounded for our transgressions, [he was] bruised for our iniquities: the chastisement of our peace [was] upon him;"

God is the author of forgiveness. Psalms 130:3-4, "If thou, Lord, shouldest mark iniquities, O Lord, who shall stand? But [there is] forgiveness with thee, that thou mayest be feared." Forgiveness was God's idea. You do not have the right to withhold forgiveness nor prostitute it for the price of vengeance.

God commands we forgive as we have been forgiven. Ephesians 4:32, "And be ye kind one to another, tenderhearted, forgiving one another, even as God for Christ's sake hath forgiven you." Matthew 6:13-14, "For if ye forgive men their trespasses; your heavenly Father will also forgive you: But if ye forgive not men their trespasses, neither will your Father forgive your trespasses." Forgiveness relinquishes the need to be right or have its own way. God was right and you were in the wrong, yet He paid the price for your forgiveness.

Forgiveness is a fruit of spiritual growth. When a fruit tree is put in the ground, it has to face rainstorms, hot sun, and strong winds. If a young tree could talk, it might say, Please get me out of here! Put me in a place where there is no sweltering heat or windy storms!" If the gardener listened to the tree, he would actually harm it. Trees endure the hot sun and rainstorms by sending their roots down deeper. The adversity they face is eventually the source of great stability (Bevere 2004).

Psalms 3:1 describes such a person. A believer who chooses to delight in the Word of God in the midst of adversity will avoid being offended. This will mature him or her to the point where adversity will now be the catalyst for fruit and usefulness to God (Bevere 2004).

Don't become a spiritual vagabond. In Gen. 4:11-12, Cain is offended at God's rejection of his gift and the consequences of his sin and recognizes that he is a vagabond (homeless; unsettled; uncertain). If a person does not mature in this area, they become a spiritual vagabond, wandering from place to place, ministry to ministry, suspicious and afraid that others will mistreat them. Soon they take on the spirit of paranoia that everyone is out to destroy their service to God. No one in ministry can be trusted except them, of course. This is where God needs their assistance in setting others straight and protecting them from being offended. They deserve not to be offended because they are on a crusade for Christ. Is this you? Keep in mind, "We will be judged according to fruit, not gifting. A gift is given. Fruit is cultivated" (Bevere 2004). Learning to cultivate forgiveness should begin in family.

Just because someone is a family member does not mean you have the liberty to offend. I have often said that one's ability to be easily offended, or offended at all, is a measuring stick of their spiritual maturity in Christ. A child is easily offended; a father is not.

There is no such thing as a completely non-dysfunctional family. Even David, being a man with a heart tested by God, and being found with a heart after

God, still had a dysfunctional family because of his sin against God. As long as we battle our sinful nature, or the sinful nature of others, there will be dysfunction. You will always find fault if that is what you are looking for. But if you allow God to change your heart and surrender to the nature of the Spirit of Christ, the battle is won and dysfunction has no power in your life or the life of your family.

Beware of those who fuel the fires of discontentment and offense for the sake of your welfare and calling. Proverbs 26:20 illustrates, "Where there is no wood, the fire goes out; and where there is no talebearer, strife ceases." People may say, "I know you are a man of God. I know God wants to do great things with you. You are being held back. Let them do their thing and we'll do ours." Offended people react to the situation and do things that appear right although God does not inspire them. A tainted conscience confuses the character of God with the compromise of men. We are not called to react but to act. God calls use to serve a higher call, one of nobility, integrity and honor. Words not often used in the English language, much less ministry, today and words that have seemingly lost any content or meaning in our culture today. Taking up another's offense; The Greek word for "offend" in Luke 17:1 comes from the word *skandalon*. This word originally referred to the part of the trap to which the bait was attached (Bevere 2004). It is only when gold is transformed into its liquid form through fire that its impurities are revealed.

In 1 Samuel 26:8, it appears that Abishai gives David very spiritually valid reasons to take the life of Saul. He presents the case that God has prepared the opportunity so that David's season of leadership could come as the Prophet Samuel had anointed him for. In deed he was partially correct. God had presented the opportunity but not for the same reason as Abishai perceived. Listen to David's response in 1 Samuel 26:9-11, "Do not destroy him; for who can stretch out his hand against the Lord's anointed, and be guiltless?...as the Lord lives, the Lord shall strike him, or his day shall come to die, or he shall go out to battle and perish. The Lord forbid that I should stretch out my hand against the Lord's anointed."

Even though information may be factual and accurate, motives are impure. Proverbs 6:16-19 says that "Sowing discord or separation among brethren is an abomination to the Lord" (Bevere 2004).

God wanted to see if David would be a leader after the heart of Saul or after the heart of righteousness. God wanted to reveal whether David still had the noble heart of a shepherd or the insecurity of another Saul. God tests His servants with obedience. He deliberately places us in situations where the standards of religion and society would appear to justify our actions. He allows others, especially those close to us, to encourage us to protect ourselves (Bevere 2004). He will also place those with critical, judgmental, and negative attitudes to see how we as His servants respond. Judas and Peter are a couple other examples. Len Ballenger says, "Jesus offended both but each responded quite differently" (Ballenger 2013).

Offended people believe everyone is out to get them. With this attitude, it is difficult for them to see areas in their own lives that need change. They think that all who do not agree with them are wrong and are against them. They isolate themselves and conduct themselves in such a manner that invites abuse (Bevere 2004). Much of it is self-induced or afflicted. Proverbs 18:1 says, "A man who isolates himself seeks his own desire; he rages against all wise judgment."

"Physical growth is a function of time. Intellectual growth is a function of learning and acquiring knowledge. Spiritual growth is neither a function of time or learning, but it is a function of obedience" (Bevere 2004).

Paul speaks of the immaturity of Christians in 2 Tim. 3:7. They have been in the church for years, can quote Scripture and many sermons but still wear spiritual diapers. Every time they meet with difficult situations, (especially in regards to relationship and authority), rather than responding by the Spirit of God, they seek to protect and defend themselves in their own way in which they have learned. They are "always learning to defend with the truth and never able to come to the knowledge of the truth in their own lives" (Bevere 2004).

How we view our past relations will determine the scope of future ones. The way you leave a church or a relationship is the way you will enter your next church or relationship. This is why many who go through a divorce are likely to go through many more; because they carry this baggage of perceptions of one bad relationship to another and another. Christ-like love forgets wrongs so there is hope for the future. Many times, God will allow people to run from situations He desires them to face if they are set on running from them in their hearts anyway. Jesus said that offenses would come. Trials and tests locate a person. In other words, they determine where you are spiritually. They reveal the true condition of your heart. How you react under pressure, disappointment, accountability or offense is how the real you reacts (Bevere 2004).

Forgiving others in Christ is not optional. It is a must. It is not one of the options on God's big drive-thru menu. It is a commandment, not a suggestion. Forgiveness for the true Christian must become a lifestyle with or without restitution. Justice does not belong to you; it belongs to God. Forgiveness is not a feeling; it is a willful and obedient choice. It is to choose God's way and not your own. In Matthew 18:21-22, Peter is proud that he had forgiven someone seven times. In that time, it was believed that the requirement ended at three according to Amos 1:3-13. Jesus' response is making reference to Genesis 4:24. Jesus was not presenting a math equation but the intent of the Law of God as God had forgiven Cain and Israel. Lamech had transgressed God's law by his polygamy and then had killed a man but justified it by God's grace to Cain. Jesus was informing Peter that His forgiveness comes not through the letter of the Law but the intent of the Law. Forgiveness is not a number but a heart condition.

One day I was studying and the Holy Spirit took me to the book of Jonah. Jonah was a prophet of God who was called to take a call of repentance to the people of Nineveh. Due to Jonah's personal offense against these people, he chose to disobey God. In Jonah Chapter 1:1-4 the Scripture tells us that Jonah fled from the "presence" of God. The word "presence" in Hebrew is *paniym* which is the same word used in Genesis 1 when the Spirit of God was upon the "face" of the deep and in Exodus when God spoke to Moses "face-to-face" or *paniym al paniym*. The Hebraic concept is one of passionate intimacy like a passionate kiss or where one is so close and consumed in unity or *echad* that it takes your breath away. In essence, Jonah was denying God intimacy. He was not just running from a task, but denying the intimate fellowship with God that comes through obedience to God. He was also denying others this same intimacy with God because of his rebellion. The passage goes on to say that as a result of Jonah's choice to rebel against God, God hurled a great storm. Now when I read this one day, God stopped me at "hurled" and said, "What does that mean today in your culture? I said, "Lord, it means to make one sick at his stomach to the point of vomiting." The Lord said to me, "Son that is exactly what happens to My heart, to Me, when My people have replaced My intimacy with entertainment in and of the church. My stomach is turned when My people deny Me the intimacy I desire with them." You would think that a prophet of God would know better. This is the power of offense and unforgiveness. Jonah held great offense against the Assyrian city and its inhabitants, both as an enemy and a personal offense, as a wicked people. However, His offense was less a means of zealousness for God's righteousness and more of his own personal prejudice of who deserved grace and who did not. When we live in offense and set ourselves up as judges against others, we separate ourselves against the intimacy of God. When you use terms like "those people", we segregate ourselves, not only from them, but from the grace of God. I have even heard professing Christians use such terms as "those homeless," "those people on...," "those whites; those blacks; those Mexicans, those homosexuals, etc." This is the root of the same attitude and language that Hitler used when he convinced others (even professing Christians) that "those Jews" were homeless vagabonds that did not want to work and were just mooching off of everyone else. People began to say, "We need to do something about "those people." It is a statement that feeds offense. As Christians, we must remember that all of "those people" need Christ Jesus. Those sinners need salvation too. Remember that you were once one of "those sinners."

How can we say we love Christ, but walk in unforgiveness? We are called to live a lifestyle of forgiveness. It is critical to our faith. Hebrews 11:6 says, "But without faith it is impossible to please God."

A lot of Christians have developed their own definition of faith. For some, it is to be on the membership of a church; for others, it is to possess great wealth and success in this life. Unfortunately, neither the prophets, Jesus, nor the Apostles defined it in any measure of those terms. Throughout Hebrews 11 you see the pattern of faith as one of belief and obedience. You cannot tell me you believe something if you do not live it. Your choices, behavior, and nature will flow out of the virtues and values of your heart and thinking. By faith (belief and obedience) Abraham laid Isaac on the altar. He acted in obedience because he valued God more than anything and trusted that God was even able to raise his son from the ashes to keep His promise. In a Hebrew sacrifice you not only cut the throat of the sacrifice, drained the blood, and placed blood on the four corners but you also burnt the sacrifice. Abraham had full intent to go through with the full sacrifice, not a partial one. If this is faith, let's look at a Scripture often quoted by many Christians who are pretty confident of their faith. Hebrews 11:1, "Now faith is the substance of things hoped for, the evidence of things not seen." Today, the church uses this as foundational to the "name it and claim it"; "give me more stuff" theology. As Pastor Lindell Ballenger once said, "True biblical prosperity is when you have everything God deems necessary to complete that which He has called you to do" (2011). But let's look at it from a Hebraic perspective. Keep in mind that the Hebrew reads from right to left and often in conceptual chunks instead of

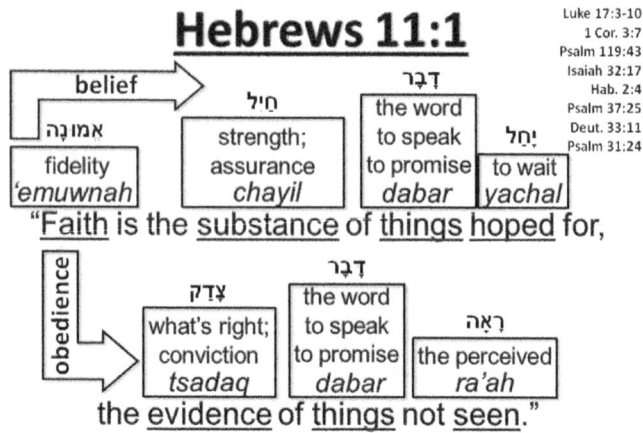

Though unperceived, the Word convicts one to wait on the promises confirmed through fidelity.

necessarily word for word. As well, to ensure contextual continuity, consider that there may, for example, be several words for "evidence" but the context depends on what the evidence produces. In the case of Hebrews 11:1, the evidence produces conviction and one does what is righteous in the eyes of God. The word faith is *'emuwnah* אֱמוּנָה which means fidelity such as in a monogamous covenant relationship. God desires and requires from His people an intimate relationship of undistracted devotion. Anything less is considered unfaithfulness, idolatry, or relational adultery. The Greek word for "substance" is *hypostasis* ὑπόστασις meaning real being; nature; foundation; assurance. It relates to the assurance of God and His faithfulness (*aman* אָמַן) and us holding fast to that which we believed in the beginning as God was in the beginning and always shall be. The Hebrew word for the Lord's substance (Deut. 33:11) is *chayil* חַיִל meaning strength; might; ability; efficiency relating to His nature and the assurance; hope; trust; and confidence in His faithfulness. The word "things" is *dabar* דָּבָר referring to a spoken word or promise. In this case, it is referring to the Word or promises of God. The entire book of Hebrews is pointing us to the promise of God to Abraham, which at its core, is the unseen presence of God dwelling within man instead of in temples. Next is the word *yachal* יָחַל (Ps. 31:24) which means to wait to trust with great expectation. The word evidence is *cephar* סֵפֶר referring to instruction; written order; legal documentation; prophetic declaration. Contextually, it is referring to the proof of God's purchase of you through Christ. Thus, it is Christ who is the evidence that you have been made *tsadaq* צָדַק (justified; made righteous) and His Spirit that produces conviction that manifest in one doing what is righteous in the eyes of God. This is why you cannot say you believe something, when it is not evident in the choices you make or the way you live your life and treat others. Thus, two key elements of true faith are belief and obedience. Finally, the Hebrew word for "seen" is *ra'ah* רָאָה. According to Dr. Ron Moseley, this speaks to the attribute of God being one who reveals. The word means that which is perceived (Moseley 2014). In this case, it is in the negative sense or that which is not perceived (Hebrews 11:13). If we conceptually look at this from a Hebraic perspective, it speaks to us that though unperceived, the Word of God convicts, or should convict one, to trustingly wait on the promises of God while remaining steadfast, confirming their faith, through the fidelity of intimate relationship with God. So it was with Abraham, according to Hebrews 11:19. To truly appreciate this concept, we must throw out the Hollywood image of Abraham standing over Isaac with a dagger about to thrust it into his belly. Even in the day of Abraham there were specific details in how sacrifices were offered to Jehovah. The altar was square. The sacrifice was to be bound, it's throat cut, the blood drained and placed on the four corners of the altar. Douglas Wheeler states that the corners represented the Father, Spirit, and Son. And the fourth corner was for you. You were to be (and had to be) an active participant in the sacrifice (Wheeler 2014). Finally, the sacrifice was to be burned. Abraham most assuredly, if he was going to be obedient to God, was not going to be halfway obedient. He had full intention of making a full and complete sacrifice to God. His expectation or faith was that God was able to raise his son even from the burnt ashes, even as Adam was created from the dust of the earth. Most of our life issues and dysfunction can be traced back to sin and our lack of Christ's Lordship in our lives. We want to go straight to the blessings and gifts of God but bypass sacrifice.

What does this have to do with relationships? Hebrews 11:6 says, "But without faith it is impossible to please Him". In Luke 17:5, the disciples ask Yeshua to increase their faith (belief and obedience to the Word of God and the intimate relationship with God). What was it that Jesus had just commanded them that provoked such a passionate request? His commandment was forgiveness. In 1 Corinthians 3 the Apostle Paul speaks concerning the same matter of dealing with that which causes division and strife. You cannot have relationship without forgiveness. Matthew 6:15 tells us that if we will not forgive others, neither will God forgive us. I am so amazed at how many Christians overlook or refuse to acknowledge this critical principle of their faith. You cannot say you have faith and relationship with God without forgiveness. I don't care how many people have been healed in your ministry; how accurate your prophecies are; or how wealthy you say God has made you. If you do not live a life of sacrificial relationship in forgiveness, you do not know God. Forgiveness is a contract between a transgressor who repents and the one violated who forgives. An exchange is made in covenant agreement that the trespass will not be repeated and the offense will not be held against the violator. The Biblical Hebraic concept of repentance is found in the word *teshuvah* תשובה. It means to return or to turn and go the other direction and never go back; to never willfully repeat the offense; or never go back to that old lifestyle or nature of sin. It is found in the parable Jesus gave of the prodigal son in Luke 15:11-32. Notice that the Father did not stand and wait for the son to reach him once he saw him. Instead, he ran to his son and met him where he was. God will meet you where you are but you have to show up to the meeting. Next, the father did not turn around and go to the past sinful life and hang out with him nor did they stay there in the present condition. Instead, the father walked with him back to the father's house where the son would be restored. Finally, the father clothed him. He placed the nicest woven robe or coat (*kethoneth* כֻּתֹּנֶת – long shirt-like garment of linen like Joseph's in Genesis 37:3) on him and covered his filth, restoring his identity as a son. Then the ring was placed on his finger. This was not just any ring but probably the signet (*chowtham* חוֹתָם) of his father. This was reserved for the elect ("chosen"; *bachar* בָּחַר) and first born as in Haggai 2:23. Then he placed new shoes (*na'al* נַעַל) on his feet. There was a Jewish custom where you took your shoes off in the presence of authority as a sign of humility and relinquishment of one's own dignity. To have your shoes removed (*halitza; ha'naal; halitzat ha'naal* – Jewish Talmudic ceremonies involving the removal of the shoes) was to be dispossessed (see Deut. 25:9; Ruth 4:7). It was part of preparing yourself to receive instruction for redemption or blessings to come your way. As well, the shoe was often used as a symbol for the transference of dominion and deliverance from past condition (Maimonides 1974). This gives further insight as to why Moses removed his shoes in the presence of God and Joshua removed his shoes in Joshua 5:15. The prodigal came with repentant heart and father embraced him with restored identity and dominion as a son.

Repentance is the first step to being human (created in the Image of God) again. To sin is not human but to be less than what God created you to be. Repentance is more than a religious concept of "Getting right with God." It is about finding who you really are and were meant to be in Christ Jesus. Without it, you are cut off from the purpose of God for your life. Without purpose, there is no real life. To be in God's image is to be purposeful about God's intentions for me. To not know God's intentions, or to know and not pursue, is to miss His image; miss His purpose and live outside of His presence. Repentance is more than confession for forgiveness. It must be followed by atonement and transformation. Regret is not repentance. It is remorse for self and the choices you made, but it does not redirect future choices. You might be more careful but there has been no change in heart. Repentance is a transformation affecting your moral compass and perspective of relationship with God (Pratney 1998). Today I hear a lot of people say that Jesus taught tolerance. What they really mean is that they want a Jesus that does not call them to repentance. Jesus taught repentance as a response to the love of the Father. Many Christians are confronted with the challenge of, "Well what if your child told you they were gay?" Many Christian struggle for an answer. As a loving father I would have the same response to any sin my child was in, I would call them to repentance. Anything less would be to respond as Eli did to his sons sin which cost them all their lives. God is calling His Bride back to her true identity in Him. He is coming back for a mature, clean, monogamously intimate Bride; one who has not taken His name just to remove her reproach, ease her conscience, and fill her coffers, but one that embraces His covenant relationship and Kingdom rule. Pastor Len Ballenger says that when Jesus called Judas out at his complaining of the woman wasting the expensive fragrance, it set in motion his offense against Jesus that later led to betrayal (Ballenger 2014). Judas could afford the offense because he had provisions for failure stashed back. However, when Jesus called Peter out to test his response for offense, Peter was restored by the question, "Do you love Me?" Do you? Do you love Him? Is your love for Him greater than your offense against your neighbor? What would be your response if Jesus called you out for your heart?

Motives and Trust

Have you ever placed your trust in someone relationally and that trust was broken? Maybe it was infidelity in a marriage covenant or maybe you shared your heart with someone and it came back to you in gossip or offense. Too often we put our trust in people instead of putting all of our trust in God. When we feel that our trust was broken by others, we tend to raise emotional and relational walls, guard our hearts, and resolve to never avail ourselves to such relational opportunities again.

The first thing I learned when I began in youth ministry was in a statement from Paul Vines who said, "You will get your heart broken and probably more than once. But it is the same with the Father, and like the Father you must continue to put your heart out there at the risk of being broken that they may know the love of the Father" (Vines 1990).

Think about how many times you have broken Father God's heart. I remember when I was younger and at a bar outside of a military base, the Lord spoke to me and said, "Son, I am going to show your earthly father where you are and what you are doing." I said, "Lord, please do not do that. I love my father and that would break his heart." And God replied, "What about my heart son?"

I have learned to put my hope and trust in Christ and not in the flesh of people. I trust in the faithfulness and goodness of God, not humanity. When I do this, through God's grace and mercy, I learn to see and trust Christ in people, looking beyond their flesh. I can then build relationship with Christ in others and when they fail, it's not me they fail. With the grace of God, I can admonish them to the Christ within. We must learn to see Christ in one another and to know each other after the Spirit of Christ and not after the flesh. (For clarification, this is not the same concept of "Christ within" as the demonic heresies of Christian Science and Scientology which are not Christian at all.)

You cannot have right relationship without trust. When trust is broken, we begin to question one another's motives. Trust is often broken as a result of living through the flesh. When we live in the flesh and begin to question other's motives instead of letting our first thought be love, trust can be destroyed. Either way, when motives and intent are questioned, the relationship begins to be poisoned. The process usually begins with the personal thought that the other is only looking out for them. We need to look out for ourselves when selfish thinking is the root of the problem. Charles Spurgeon said that most people serve God out of two motivations – fear of punishment or hope of reward – and both are selfish. We want to avoid correction, punishment or consequences, but reap personal satisfaction, benefit, and gratification or gain (Pratney 1998). At some point in our life, if we do not grow past this, we will never have healthy relationships. When we grow to a mature love and things do not work out the way we think they should, the relationship is not shaken. Your love for Father has to be built on more than what He does or does not do for you. He is not your negatively stereotyped step dad or divorced father who feels the need to buy your love. He has already bought it and paid the highest price with His Son Jesus Christ. Too often, we question God's motives and love for us when we are going through trials or correction and wonder if He still loves us. This is childish, as John describes in 1 John 2:12-14. Prophet Kevin Leal says that most of what is preached or sung today is focused on reassuring us that God still loves us, even when we sin because the Body of Christ is not growing up. We are not growing up because of apostasy. There is rampant apostasy because we have generations without real discipleship. We want to have church void of sacrificial relationship. As a result, we question motives through our assumptions that are driven by emotion. As well, we misjudge, not because of the other person, but because of our own heart condition. Most relationship issues come back to an issue of Lordship. Somewhere, Christ is not Lord--- someone or something else is.

Philippians 2:3 tells us, "Let nothing be done through selfish ambition or conceit, but in lowliness of mind let each esteem others better than himself." Proverbs 16:18, "Pride goes before destruction and a haughty spirit before a fall." Both of these passages are speaking to the motives of the heart. The wrong motives bring destruction and death but the right motives bring life. In James 5:16, it says, "Confess your trespasses to one another, and pray for one another, that you may be healed." The point is to make reconciliation (forgiveness, repentance, and restitution) a common practice in your relationships so that you and your relationships may be healthy and whole. What does he mean "confess your trespasses or sins to one another"? If you have an offense against one another, go to one another quickly and reconcile. Do not wait days and harbor offense, building increased offense through vain imagination, anger, and deceit until the relationship is destroyed. Dig up the seeds of division quickly before it takes root. Scripture says that we should go to them face to face before the Sun goes down. Nowhere in Scripture does it say to text them with your offense and say some snide remark about the situation in deceitful code on your Facebook page. There is nothing worse than trying to deal with offense over text and email. It is ungodly, unbiblical, unhealthy and extremely unfruitful. In fact, a phone call is not even much better. If the relationship ever meant anything and if you really want to honor God, then make the time and effort to meet face to face. Texting, Facebooking, Tweeting--- all of these undetached and impersonal methods do not bring healing and are a form of immaturity and irresponsibility when it comes to reconciling offenses. Dealing with conflict this way is often an easy way out, a devaluing of personal relationship, and a cowardice way of confronting problems with one another. If you have a problem with me, come to me face to face and give me the chance to show you how much I love you by offering peace and reconciliation. You cannot see my love in a text message but when you have to look me in the eyes, you might see Christ more than your offense. We live in a time now where people want Godly Biblical counseling for things like their marriage over a text, email, social media or blog page. This is so unhealthy for the Body of Christ and we are seeing the results as people are not growing or maturing relationally in the family.

Matthew 18:15 says to "go to your brother" and reconcile between you and he alone. The implication here is not to go tell him what an evil sinner he is and how he did you dirty. The point is to go with the motive and intent to restore the relationship where both of you can honor God with your hearts. It might even be that you take the mature road, humble yourself, and ask how have I offended you or what have I done that something is hindering our hearts? In Matthew 5:39, Jesus uses a Hebraic idiom "to turn the other cheek". He was not implying Christian pacifism. The principle was in line with the rest of the context. It was not to retaliate and return evil for evil. This commonly understood idiom meant that if your brother had not spoken of you in over three days, you were to take the higher moral, mature, relational ground by humbling yourself and going to him for reconciliation. It stressed responding to conflict with humility.

When you doubt someone's motives, begin to earnestly pray for them out of the love of Christ. It will begin to change your heart. However, you cannot pray for them with the wrong motives, "Lord, bless that evil sucker and reveal to them the error of their ways and the demons they are full of. Lord, don't judge them for what they did to me and cause some kind of sickness Lord. Well, at least nothing that will kill them Lord." This is what I call Jesus JuJu or Christian Voodoo; or what my friend, Pastor Len Ballenger, calls Christian Curses (Ballenger 2012). Instead, pray, "Lord, help me to love as You love. Help me not to misjudge or question their motives. Lord, help me to know them after their heart and not their flesh. Help me Lord, to be gracious and understand that we might be healed and reconciled." When we learn to follow these principles, we can have healthy and whole relationships instead of being satisfied with partial and superficial relationships with one another and with God. We can also allow God to heal us of the broken relationships of our past.

2 Corinthians 4:16-18 states, "Therefore we do not lose heart. Even though our outward man is perishing, yet the inward man is being renewed day by day. For our light affliction, which is but for a moment, is working for us a far more exceeding and eternal weight of glory, while we do not look at the things which are seen, but at the things which are not seen. For the things

which are seen are temporary, but the things which are not seen are eternal."

Again, your soul is eternal and you were created for eternal relationship. When you stand before God, you will account for what you said (Matthew 12:36); what you have done (Revelations 20:12); and our thoughts and motives (Hebrews 4:12). All of these are tied to our relationships with one another and with God. Therefore, relationships are eternal and we will account for our part in our relationships whether good or bad. It will not be about who was wrong or right but who honored the way of the Lord and held fast to their integrity in Christ. We must keep our focus and attention on that which is eternal. Remember, we fight not against flesh and blood. These are temporary. But the spirit, the souls of men and the Word of God are eternal.

The flesh man will perish but the inward man is eternal. Through Christ, the inward man can be renewed, strengthened and grow in the nature and maturity of Christ in day by day communion in the Spirit and Word of God. God never said that conflicts and afflictions would not come in this life, but if we learn to live and know Him and each other after the Spirit, then these will be but light afflictions that increase the measure of His glory in our lives.

The disciples had to learn to know Christ after the Spirit rather than just after the flesh. They only thought they knew Him while they walked with Him. But after He was crucified and buried, they had to learn how to know Him after the Spirit. Peter convinced himself that he truly knew Christ, but when he was faced with preserving his own life or denying his knowing Jesus, he emphatically declared, "I do not know Him" three times. On the third denial, I believe that Peter got a revelation: He really did not know Christ as he thought he did. Doubting, Thomas had to touch Him to believe, but Jesus said, "…blessed are those who believe and have not seen Me." Jesus was saying, "Blessed are those who know Me after the Spirit." When the Scripture says in Genesis 2:24 that "a man shall leave his father and mother and cleave unto his wife and the two shall become one," it is talking about knowing each other after the spirit that they are *echad* or in unity, even in the flesh. It's like a husband and wife who have been together so long they can finish one another's sentences; they know how the other thinks; they sense one another's emotions to the point they may even begin to take on features of one another's countenance from sharing the same emotional traits. They have grown beyond knowing one another's habits but they have grown to know each other's spirits which makes for a deeper and richer relationship. Habits become less significant, even if they are annoying ones, because the love is deeper and richer than habits.

The Apostle Paul had not known Christ after the flesh but only after the Spirit. Thus, he states in 2 Corinthians 5:14-16, "For the love of Christ compels us, because we judge thus: that if One died for all, then all died; and He died for all, that those who live should live no longer for themselves, but for Him who died for them and rose again. Therefore, from now on, we regard no one according to the flesh. Even though we have known Christ according to the flesh, yet now we know Him thus no longer."

We too must learn to know God after the Spirit of Christ. Our trusting in Him, our love for Him, our motives of obedience must grow to a maturity where we do not trust, obey and love Him because we have seen Him, or for what He can do to us or for us, but because we *'ahabah, da'ath, and yada'* Him after the inward man through the knowledge of the Holy Spirit.

If I truly love God and love you, then when thoughts or feelings of questionable motives come, they are quickly dispelled by love. The goal is to always let my first thought be love.

Likewise, we must learn to have relationship with one another not by what we know of each other's sinful nature, faults, and failures; not by what others can give me or do for my own selfish motives, but to know each other after the redeemed nature of Christ; after the love of the Spirit of God; after the will of the Father to glorify not ourselves but He who has called us unto Himself for purity and unity of heart in relationship. If we will learn to live by these principles as God says to live, then they will guard our hearts and we can live in right relationship. I believe they will bring healing to our children, our marriages, our families, the Body of Christ, and ultimately, will impact our nation.

If our relationships are built solely on our carnal nature instead of the redeemed nature through Christ, then there will never be security in the relationship. We have to get beyond knowing each other after our faults, failures, and sinful natures; what someone else can do for us; and our own selfish motives. We must know each other after the Spirit of Christ Jesus. When each in the relationship is operating out of this heart, mind and motive, Christ is the center of the relationship and God is glorified. Instead of being offended at faults, I show grace, respond with love, and the Holy Spirit helps me grow up in the stature of Jesus Christ.

How important are our motives to God concerning relationships? Proverbs 16:2 says, "All the ways of a man are pure in his own eyes, but the LORD weighs the spirits." And in 1 Corinthians 4:5, "Therefore judge nothing before the time, until the Lord comes, who will both bring to light the hidden things of darkness and reveal the counsels of the hearts. Then each one's praise will come from God." In James 2 verse 4, it says, "…have you not shown partiality among yourselves, and become judges with evil thoughts?" And finally in Hebrews 4:12 we are told, "For the word of God is living and powerful, and sharper than any two-edged sword, piercing even to the division of soul and spirit, and of joints and marrow, and is a discerner of the thoughts and intents of the heart." All of these passages are referring to God's knowing and judging the motives of our hearts. You may not like this, but in every relationship, God knows and is keeping record of your motives and intentions. You might say, "But I thought the Bible said that God does not remember my sins?" It says in Hebrews 8:12, quoting Jeremiah 31:34, "For I will be merciful to their unrighteousness, and their sins and their lawless deeds I will remember no more." The Hebrew word for "remember" is *zakar* זָכַר and means to call to remembrance; to be brought to mind; or to record. So, it does not mean to that God has amnesia but chooses not to recall or He chooses to remove from the record those sins for which you repent. When you gossip, there's a record. So, when you leave relationships with unresolved or open ended offenses and sins and continue with an unrepentant heart and enmity against another, there is a record until you repent. Only when you repent and live in right relationship with God are your sins remembered no more. Before God said in Jeremiah 31:34 that He would remember your sins no more, He also said, "…and they will *know (yada')* Me." But that is not how we live in the church today. It is not how we deal with relationships. We live as if we are justified with every offense as we disconnect, de-friend, move from church family to church family doing our thing in the Lord. Forgiveness over comes that which you have true repentance of. The antinomian idea that God keeps no record of my sins anymore so I can live however I want is a problem of the heart's motive and is rooted in more love of hedonistic self-pleasures than an obedient and honorable love for God.

It is by the motives and intentions of our hearts that God judges each of us. God's motives are always for:

1. The Honor of His name (Isaiah 6:3)
2. The Reconciliation of His people (2 Corin. 5:18)
3. Intimate relationship with you (John 17:23)
4. The preparing holiness of His Bride (Rev. 21:2)
5. The establishing of His Kingdom (Isaiah 9:7)

All too often, we misjudge people's motives without forethought and due consideration. We many times criticize others unfairly without consideration of what we do not know. Instead, we judge based on what we presume we know about others and their situation. Have you ever experienced a situation where someone you knew suddenly had a significant personality and attitude shift? And your response was to be offended and disconnect only to find out a few months later that they were diagnosed with a brain tumor? Well, I have. I did not disconnect relationally but I did learn a major lesson in life. I learned that I do not have time for offenses and childish, selfish immaturity. I have been given just enough time in this life to love God and others with all my heart, soul, mind and strength regardless of circumstances. Man has searched throughout history for the meaning to life. I have discovered that life is one short journey to intimately get to know my Creator in preparation for eternity with Him. Therefore, we must remember foremost the years of great relationship we have had with people and when something in the relationship changes, love them enough to be slow to judge and quick to have grace. If the relational motive is love, you can quickly recognize that something is wrong and maybe even save their life. If you have known them after the Spirit, then when something changes in the flesh, you can recognize it and intervene.

There is no better illustration than the way we often misjudge the motives and so quickly destroy the trust of relationship with those we should know better than anyone else, and that is our own family members. With family, we often times think we have relationship simply because they may live in the same house, but in reality, we may only have familiarity. As a result, we fail to have grace for family. How can you live in the same house, speak with someone day after day, and still miss-judge their motives towards you or in what they say and do. It is simply because of sin. God can judge motives because He is without sin. If you are convinced that you are without sin, you probably have a nice stone collection and a good arm. Jesus told the Pharisees who brought the accused adulterous woman to be stoned without any opportunity for repentance, "Let you without sin throw the first stone (John 8:7)," He was saying, "Who are you to judge without repentance?" However, we are not God and sin impairs our judgment. This does not mean we are not to judge at all. To not judge at all would mean to live lawless; to never discipline our children; to never call into question ones character. We make judgments every day. It means we are not to judge by our own standard or opinion but to judge according to the Law, character, and nature of God. To not call sin by its first name because of the plank in my own eye is foolish. I just need to first repent and pull the plank out of my own eye then in love help my brother, through the Spirit of Christ, remove speck in his eye. So, how does this apply to bringing reconciliation with a family member? The same way God says to bring reconciliation with others.

If someone has sinned against you or you are aware of their sinful habits, choices, or condition, it is easy to judge the motives of their heart as sinful in the entirety of their life and relationships. But we must consider, even still, that the person may desire to be free from sin but does not know how or is struggling to be free. Ours, then, is to seek to reconcile them in the grace of God to the righteousness of Christ. Often in the church we think this means to just overlook their sinful rebellion; to tolerate it and call that grace, hoping that someday they may come to the revelation of their wicked ways. But this is not how God says to truly bring them into reconciliation with God. The goal is less about being reconciled to you, your opinion, your bias, your theology, your doctrine or your preference but about you and them being reconciled in righteous relationship with God. Sin separates us from relationship with God.

In Matthew 18:15-17, Jesus gives us a clear itinerary for bringing reconciliation. Yet, I am amazed at how we want to either sit piously in church or come and juke and jive or whoop and holler in a Holy Ghost shindig (as we say in Arkansas) but when it comes to humbling ourselves for reconciliation, we throw that out the window. Christians want to quote all the prosperity faith Scriptures, "I am the head and not the tail," "I am blessed coming in and going out; good measure pressed down, shaken together, and running over!" But when it comes to reconciliation – it's just not part of their spirituality! Scripture teaches us that if you believe or perceive that someone has wronged you, don't take the risk of misjudging the motives of their heart. Keep in mind, when you begin to judge another's heart's motive, you have stepped into a realm of being a divine judge. Instead, go to them and tell them your offense, giving them the opportunity to reconcile with your heart. If they refuse to listen to you, then there is a bigger problem of the hearts and relationship with God. Take those with you who have spiritual authority over you both. Neither Jesus nor Paul taught for you to gather you an offense posse and go attack them. They do not say go share some gossip about the other person. And if you are a leader in the church, sitting and entertaining gossip about other leaders is not considered Biblical Counseling but partaking in gossip and division. There is no such thing as gossip with the intent to reconcile. Instead, use the spiritual leadership which God has placed you under. If there still cannot be reconciliation, then the leaders are to bring it before the entire congregation and address the issue that all may be reconciled and no further division come of it. In 2 Thessalonians 3:14-15, it states, "And if anyone does not obey our word in this epistle, note that person and do not keep company with him, that he may be ashamed. Yet do not count him as an enemy, but admonish him as a brother." And I Corinthians 5:11-13,

"But now I have written to you not to keep company with anyone named a brother, who is sexually immoral, or covetous, or an idolater, or a reviler, or a drunkard, or an extortioner - not even to eat with such a person. For what have I to do with judging those also who are outside? Do you not judge those who are inside? But those who are outside God judges. Therefore put away from yourselves the evil person." Put those who refuse to repent under the grace of God, out of the fellowship, that God may judge them unto reconciliation and repentance. I have confronted issues such as gossip and division in the House of the Lord and had people say, "Well, this is just between me and my disgruntled family members." I don't care if it is dysfunction in your immediate or extended family. If you are a part of the church family, I have been given responsibility by God and you will repent, reconcile, and end the gossip according to the Word of God or leave. If one family is unhealthy, the whole house is either unhealthy or soon will be. Unfortunately, this level of accountability is not often in the Body of Christ or people do not want it. As a result, church buildings grow but families do not. Instead, the divorce rate, porn addictions and everything else grows even faster than the building funds. It never fails that someone will come to me asking, "Pastor, what happened to so and so. I have not seen them at church." When all the while I know they have been talking to them or reading their comments on their social media. I warn you, do not entertain the gossip of social media among those who have the spirit of division.

We should always allow love to believe the best. The door of reconciliation should always be open. We should always give opportunity to ensure that the motives of our hearts are in the way of the Lord in any situation. We should never be too quick to judge one's motives until we have done all due diligence to reconcile the relational situation. Pastor Dennis Pratt once told me, "Never judge based on personality, opinion, perception, or feelings. Always judge based on the precepts and principles of righteousness, allowing the Word of God to be that which reveals the motives of the heart."

John Wesley told of a man he had little respect for because he considered him to be miserly and covetous. One day when this person contributed only a small gift to a worthy charity, Wesley openly criticized him. After the incident, the man went to Wesley privately and told him he had been living on parsnips and water for several weeks. He explained that before his conversion, he had run up many bills. Now, by skimping on everything and buying nothing for himself, he was paying off his creditors one by one. "Christ has made me an honest man," he said, "and so with all these debts to pay, I can give only a few offerings above my tithe. I must settle up with my worldly neighbors and show them what the grace of God can do in the heart of a man who was once dishonest." Wesley then apologized to the man and asked his forgiveness.

Wrong motives in our own hearts, which cause us to quickly and falsely assume the motives of others hearts, most often are the signs of the seeds of:

1. Pride (esteeming self above the glory of God)
2. Fear of losing something like a position, prestige, and personal gain
3. Greed and Envy

Wrong motives in our heart will hinder:
1. Worship
2. Prayer
3. Obedience to God
4. The will of God in your life
5. Relationships

Through obedience to Christ, relationships can be restored. We can learn to trust again, not just the motives of other's hearts but the motive of the Spirit of Christ in those who seek to please God. Through our own surrender to obedience to Christ we can learn to rightly discern the motives and intents of one another's heart because we learn to know each other after the Spirit of Christ instead of the sinful flesh that we all contend with. We can look at the fruit of one another's lives and see Christ. And when offenses come we remember the fruit of the love in Christ we have shared, instead of presumptuous misconception of the moment of offense.

Have you misjudged someone's motives? Have you judged another after the flesh instead of the Spirit of

Christ? Have you built walls because you have come to question everyone's motives and said to yourself you would never trust again? Learn to let the love of God be your guide and measure of judgment. Let the Spirit of Christ be that which you trust. Let the desire to please God with your whole heart be your motive in all things. Be reconciled first and foremost with the heart of Father that you might not live in a constant state of misperception, false judgment, and constant offense.

Look at what Scripture says about Job. Job had every right to be offended at God and his friends by our fleshly standard, but instead, he said to God, "I know that you can do all things, and that no purpose of yours can be thwarted." (Job 42:2) "And the Lord restored the fortunes of Job, when he had prayed for his friends." (Job 42:10)

When you live in obedience to the knowledge of God, you can live with assurance and confidence that the plans of God are full proof. Nothing is impossible with God. When your life is in sync with the plans and purposes of God, then those plans and purposes cannot be shaken or cut off (*batsar* בָּצַר). You get the honor and privilege of participating in the plans and purposes of God as He reveals to you who He is and what He is doing. As my friend Trey McClendon states, "It is time to watch God do what He said He would do" (McClendon 2011). When you are walking by a faith that "knows the unlimited power of Almighty God," then you have full access to the purposes of God in your life. It is through the love of the Father that nothing is inaccessible or withheld from those who seek Him with their whole heart. Nothing is too difficult when you purpose to do what God has already purposed He would do for you. When the motivation of your purpose is in alignment with the will of God, you make all things right because you love the Lord. One of the purposes of the *Yamim Noraim* ימים נוראים (Ten Days of Repentance; *teshuva* תשובה; Lev. 23:24) is the restoration of relationships. Job's supposed friends had come against him pretty hard during his time of affliction. They were not there to encourage and support but instead, they ridiculed and condemned. Yet in the end, God had done something in Job that motivated him to pray for them and lead them to repentance. When Job understood grace, Job showed grace and prayed for his friends. It was in this act of repentance and restoration that God bestowed abundantly more than Job had lost. The next time you are going through hardship or a trial in your life, remind yourself that your God can do all things. Ensure your life is in alignment with the plans and purposes of God. You can do this by getting your focus off of you and reaching out and praying for someone else, even if it is someone who may have come against you in the past. God is a God of restoration and redemption.

Marriage Matters

Genesis 2:18: "And the LORD God said, 'It is not good that man should be alone; I will make him a helper comparable to him.'" The word used in this passage for "helper" in the Hebrew is *'ezer* עֵזֶר which simply means "help meet" or "one who helps." The term "for him" in Hebrew is *neged* נֶגֶד which means "in front of or before his face." The Hebraic concept here is that God made woman to first help man in the dominion task given by God; second, to be in face-to-face relational intimacy with him through God and to be before his face as a reflection and accountability partner in life before God. Not a confrontational "in your face" relationship but a team partner in life and holiness as each admonishes the other to holiness and right relationship. Therefore, in this passage was the first marriage ordained by God.

Other than God, a man's wife should be his accountability partner. Woman was not created to simply take orders from man. God was not initiating a chauvinist order but a covenant of unity that reflected Himself to man. The idea was that woman helped man and man helped woman and together, they served God.

From the beginning, God intended for man and woman to enjoy each other's companionship in righteous covenant and serving the Lord, not themselves, together. If a husband and wife cannot serve in life together, then something is wrong. Either one or both of their hearts, attitudes, or thinking is wrong in what it means to honor and live selflessly for God or what God's perception and intent of marriage is.

In the New King James the word "comparable" is used. The point made is that each is of equal value and service to God.

Proverbs 21:9 states, "Better to dwell in a corner of a housetop, than in a house shared with a contentious woman." The word for "contentious" in the Hebrew is *midyan* מִדְיָן meaning brawling, confrontational, or full of strife. Thus, a man would rather live in the corner of the attack in his house than with a wife who likes to fuss, fight, complain, and argue all the time. Unless you want your husband to avoid you, learn to live in peace and contentment. However, before you want to tase me ladies, this applies to men as well. No good woman wants to live with a man who cannot control his anger. The Word of God is an equal opportunity offender. Ephesians 5:33 states, "Nevertheless let each one of you in particular so love his own wife as himself, and let the wife see that she respects her husband." I have found in marriage counseling that most men desire to be shown sincere respect and most women simply want to feel and intimately know the security of the relationship. Love and respect are vital aspects of any marital relationship. Although both desire love and respect, a good wife will do almost anything for a man who treats her in a sincere loving manner; one whom she can count on, trust in, and know that he is always there for her or faithful. What a woman desires to see and know is stability, consistency, and maturity in a man. She wants a man that is truly a man and not a boy in a man's body who wants the benefits of manhood but not the responsibility and accountability that comes with it. Prophet Kevin Leal calls this a "man-child." I call it the Peter Pan Syndrome. Men, don't ask God for a wife when you don't even have a job. God will not send you a spouse for you to goof up their life like yours. Get your house in order. Ladies, if his bible is not marked up, his life is probably messed up. And ladies, if you caught him by flaunting your immodest body at church, don't wonder why he has a pornography or lust problem after you are married. You did let God send him to you based on godly character in the first place.

Husbands and wives, 1 Corinthians 7:5 says, "Do not deprive one another except with consent for a time that you may give yourselves to fasting and prayer; and come together again so that Satan does not tempt you because of your lack of self-control." A lot of fathers and husbands today want sexual gratification in the marriage relationship but do not want to commit faithfully to the responsibilities of the roles that come with covenantal relational intimacy. They are not willing to make the daily self-sacrifices it takes to be a godly husband and father. They do not know when it is time to put down the video game controller; come home to meet the needs of the family instead of hanging out with the guys like a single dude; and sacrifice getting what you want to secure the provisions of the family in righteous stewardship. Yet, they want a wife to follow them, meaning do what I want when I want you to do it and take care of me like my mother did. This is not Biblical Manhood. I Corinthians 7:5 speaks of sexual intimacy but also presents a Biblical principle of selflessness in every area of your life. A husband or wife does not have the right to withhold, not only their physical intimacy, but also their affection, love, joys, or heart. They are to bring all of themselves into the relationship surrendered and holy to God for the good of God and the other that the relationships may be whole or complete, just as we have to come to Christ. Neither comes forcing their self upon the other but in an attitude of offering. This applies physically, mentally, spiritually and emotionally. Even in a marriage, you can pervert intimacy that was to be holy before God. Intimacy is to be mutual. If it is forced or coerced, it is perverted and still a form of spousal abuse or rape. If it is given quid pro quo, even among a husband and wife, it has been prostituted (such as sexual favors for spending money). Even if your wife says she is okay with your pornography addiction, God still calls it adultery. The same applies to your flirtatious nature, contacting old lovers through social media. It is all a condition of the heart. The problem is that we have come so far culturally, even in the church, that couples act like they have forgotten what normal intimacy in a covenant relationship is supposed to look like. Some couples even reach the point in their marriage that they might occasionally have sex, if the other persists enough, but they withhold their intimacy in the process. This is a sign that something is wrong in their heart. They convince themselves it's because of other issues physically, emotionally, or mentally. There may be issues hindering sexual activity but they are no excuse to withhold the affection and intimacy of your heart and soul to your spouse. Marital intimacy has to be built on more than mere sexual activity.

2 Corinthians 6:14 "Do not be unequally yoked together with unbelievers. For what fellowship has righteousness with lawlessness? And what communion has light with darkness?" This passage has been so taken out of context and used even to justify racial prejudice. However, it is talking about being spiritually unequally yoked. Two people in covenant cannot serve two different gods. If Christ is your first priority and the first love of your life, how can you make covenant with someone who does not hold the same value of your eternal passion? "When people who are committed to a particular religion choose to marry someone of another religion or no religion, they are setting the relationship up for failure. A lack of compatibility in the area of religion makes it difficult for a husband and wife to connect on the deepest level" (Livermore 2008).

Many people join in marriage yet are not only spiritually unequally yoked with one another but with the Word of God itself. They do not follow God's instruction when it comes to the communication, finances, doctrine, and even parenting. For example, Ephesians 6:1 states, "Children obey your parents in the Lord, for this is right." It has become the norm in many families for the children to dictate the running of the household; to decide their own acceptable behavior; and basically to be the ones in charge. The parents spend more time appeasing the child so as to avoid any confrontation that might inconvenience them. The Scripture makes it clear that the children are to obey the parents, not the parents obey the children. However, that which you tolerate will become intolerant of that which tolerated it. If you allow your child to talk back, swing at you, tell you "no" when told to do something, and throw tantrums at four years old, do not cry and ask why when at fourteen they are telling you where to go and what to do with yourself. When the Scriptures say in Proverbs 22:6, "Train up a child in the way he should go, And when he is old he will not depart from it." The assumption is that the parents are themselves living and training the children in the way of the Lord. When God addresses family relationships, He is not just addressing the children but He also gives instruction to the parents. The old saying that children or parenting does not come with an instruction manual is a lie. God has given plenty of instruction to both. Parents have the responsibility to witness to their children and lead them in the way of Christ and into personal and intimate relationship with God. Parents are to demonstrate the way of the Lord. Fathers are instructed to relate to their children in a way that is kind and gentle, yet firm, authoritative and absolute without scolding, demeaning, and oppressing. Ephesians 6:4 admonishes, "And you fathers, do not provoke your children to wrath, but bring them up in the training and admonition of the Lord." Fathers are to not only live as the godly prophet, priest, and king of their homes, but they are to demonstrate the nature and character of God the Father to their children. If father could not control his anger and wrath, then God must be an angry vengeful god. If father was not there for them they will grow to believe that God will not be there for them. If father was absent in the important moments of their life, why should they involve God in the important moments of their life? Parents, you do not get a vacation from parenting and parenting is not a duty, obligation, or burdensome responsibility. It has to be viewed as an honor, privilege, and gift given by God. Any other perspective will be reflective in your children. As well, what you make a priority in your life will become your children's priority as well. If it is self and personal pleasure and gratification, so it will be with them. If serving the Lord and selfless sacrifice is not a priority to you in their pre-teen years, do not be surprised when they grow to want nothing to do with the House of the Lord. You can blame it on the church; youth group wasn't cool enough or whatever. But the reality is that you did not make honoring God a priority in your life nor theirs. If you have not surrendered self completely to God then you will not have an effective relationship with your children, spouse, or anyone. Philippians 2:3 states, "Let nothing be done through selfish ambition or conceit, but in lowliness of mind, let each esteem others better than himself." Our natural, carnal, fleshly tendency is to look out for self first and foremost. But the Bible teaches that to have healthy relationship, we each must live by honoring others. Many relationships fall apart because of selfish pride. It is like a stone wall inhibiting people from confessing sin, asking forgiveness, offering apologies or opening the road blocks to reconciliation. James 5:16 tells us, "Make this your common practice: Confess your sins to each other and pray for each other so that you can live together whole and healed." In other words, James is telling us to make it a habitual practice or a natural response as part of our daily lives to confess our sins one to another. I believe the reason we do not teach our children to confess their sins is because we ourselves are unwilling to practice the same demands of the Kingdom of God. If we practiced this in reality, I guarantee you most of the offenses and arguments that divide would lose their power and we would learn to become better communicators; learn self-control; and guard our hearts and lips to prefer and protect one another's hearts. A kind word turns away wrath but angry words never produce peace but provoke more and increase anger (Proverbs 15:1). James 1:19 says, "My dear brothers and sisters, be quick to listen, slow to speak, and slow to get angry." Many times the silliest, smallest, and most insignificant things in disagreements and misinterpretations elevate and bring division and destruction. Why do we not first stop in the midst of the argument and ask ourselves if it is really worth it? Is it worth losing this relationship? What is to be gained? The answer is that we do not stop because we are so consumed and focused on self in the midst of the argument. Words of strife only produces more words of strife. Proverbs 6:19 says that God hates and considers an abomination the sowing of discord among one another. The word for discord in Hebrew is *medan* מְדָן which means strife, division, or contention.

James does not end with confession but goes on to tell us to pray for one another. If we will practice these things, they will help us to be made whole and healed. In other words, we might know and enjoy the richness and fullness of right relationship. When we honor God's ways it gives our relationships with one another the opportunity to be made whole and healthy. When we walk in humility, we can walk in reconciliation. When each of us freely admits our faults and gives grace one to another, it will improve our relationships. Healthy relationships include mutual burden bearing" (Livermore 2008).

Keep in mind that this practice of confession and repentance must be in a safe environment that has been mutually developed. James does not say confess the other persons faults to them, for them. Nor does it say make your point and cut the other person with sarcasms when they ask for forgiveness. If they ask you to forgive them for misjudging and saying the wrong things and your reply is, "I forgive you because you do it often." That does not lend to a mutual practice of the principles of God. Ephesians 4:29 states "Do not let any unwholesome talk come out of your mouth, but only what is helpful for building others up according to their needs, that it may benefit those who listen." How you speak to one another is critical to developing and sustaining a healthy relationship. Kindness and forgiveness are essential ingredients to a healthy relationship. Ephesians 4:32 says, "And be kind to one another, tenderhearted, forgiving one another, even as God in Christ forgave you." Hebrews 10:24-25 tells us to "consider one another and stir up love…" You can have all the ingredients to make a cake but you do not have a cake. You can even mix them altogether and you do not have a cake until you place it in the heat. This is the test of a relationship. When the relationship is tested and tried in the heat of conflict and opposition; trials and tribulations will prove it. Often we view conflict as a negative when actually, without conflict, there can be no change and without change, there can be no growth and maturity in the relationship. I have found that the hardships my family has faced have often brought us closer together in a stronger bond because we work together in life as a team, seeking and trusting in our hope of who Jesus Christ is. Hope in anything else is false hope. Often we say we are hoping in Christ when actually, we are just hoping in and for a different outcome or set of circumstances. However, as we hope in Christ together, we grow together in Christ. I have learned that I must daily pursue the heart of Father God. And just as Christ pursues the heart of His Bride, as Pastor Woody Tolleson puts it; so I must pursue and seek to win the heart of my wife and children daily (Tolleson 2014). Some men think that just because they won their wife's heart in marriage that they got the prize and it's time to move on to the next objective. However, God designed their hearts to be pursued by a deeper love as God desires with us. The Word of God is filled with answers to relational issues if we would just seek them out and apply them to our lives.

Study and Discussion Questions

The Building Blocks of Relationship

1. According to Deut. 7:6-9, what does it mean to have a Lordship relationship with Christ?
2. Discuss the process of Divine Fulfillment.
3. What are the three building blocks of relationship?
4. What does the word *yada'* mean in your relationship with God?
5. Discuss the contrast between what God defines as normal relationship and what the world defines as normal relationship.

Building Blocks of Family

1. What are the implications of Proverbs 4:1 in our culture today? How have these affected families?
2. What are the six Foundational Principles of Fathering? How have they impacted your life?
3. Discuss the typical motives or reasons most people enter into relationships?
4. Discuss some of the healthy safety barriers God has placed in relationships.

5. How does unnecessary drama affect our relationships? What is often the root of such drama?

Worldview of Relationships

1. According to Matthew 12:34 and Proverbs 4:23, your thoughts, words, and actions are a reflection of what? Explain.
2. Regardless of their argument, the real problem most people have with God is what? Explain.
3. What does 2 Corinthians 6:14 have to do with relationships?
4. What does God mean by the word "perfect" or in Hebrew *tamiym*? How does it apply to you and relationships in your life?
5. 1 Corinthians 13 presents the Legos of healthy relationships. Explain how they connect together to build strong and healthy relationships.
6. Discuss what a good relationship sight picture looks like from God's perspective.

Redefining Intimacy

1. How does sex outside of the covenant of marriage affect the individuals, their relationship with each other, and God?
2. How have the ideologies of humanism and hedonism affected families and internal relationships in today's society?
3. How have the ideologies of humanism, hedonism, and antinomianism affected the church today in regard to relationships?
4. True godly relationships are built on:
    a. _____

    b. _____
    c. _____
5. Explain the correlation between a husband and wife relationship relative to Christ and the Church as expressed in the Hebrew word *dabaq*.

Communications and Insecurities

1. Discuss the concept of filtering our thoughts, words, and actions through the Word of God and how it affects our relationships?
2. How does the Hebraic concept of *nachash* in Genesis 3:1 relate to Proverbs 23:7, Matthew 5:27-28, and Christ's work at the cross?
3. How does God communicate His will to us? How can we use God's method and model in our communication with others?
4. What are the seven things we all need for healthy development in our identity? How do these affect our view of and relationship to God and others?
5. Discuss the process of dialogue development as we mature from selfish to altruistic communication.

Offenses and Forgiveness

1. What is Satan's greatest bait to divide and conquer the church?
2. Describe the concept of a spiritual vagabond. Scripturally, how can we avoid this condition?
3. How have we in the church made the forgiveness of others who have offended us optional?

4. Discuss the response differences between Peter and Judas when Jesus offended them in Matthew 26:6-16 and Matthew 16:21-24.
5. Explain the danger in using terms like "those people".

Motives and Trust

1. Describe the Biblical process of reconciliation relative to today's non-personable approach to conflict resolution and use of technology.
2. What did the Hebrew idiom "turn the other cheek" really mean? How does that relate to relationships in your life?
3. How will we account to God for relationships in this life?
4. Discuss what it means to know one another after the spirit instead of the flesh.
5. What are the five things God's motives are towards? Discuss scripturally.
    a. _____
    b. _____
    c. _____
    d. _____
    e. _____
6. Wrong motives and misjudgments often stem from what seeds?

Marriage Matters

1. Discuss Genesis 2:18 in light of the Hebrew concepts of *'ezer* and *neged.*
2. How does the spiritual unity, or lack of spiritual unity, affect children in the home?

3. How does ones worldview of marriage affect family harmony and the identity of those in the home?
4. Can there be perversion of the marriage covenant? Explain.
5. Where must true and pure intimacy in a marriage flow from? Explain.
6. Is marital intimacy merely physical? How does this relate to your relationship with God? Explain.

Bibliography

Adams, Jay. *Competent to Counsel* (1970). Grand Rapids, Michigan: Zondervan Publishing House.

Barham, Johnny (1986). Relationships. Living Water Fellowship.

Battles, Keith (2012). Holy Matrimony. Found at http://www.bing.com/videos/search?q=keith+battles&qpvt=keith+battles&FORM=VDRE#view=detail&mid=CD964A4ADD1D57226ACFCD964A4ADD1D57226ACF.

Bevere, John *The Bait of Satan* (2004). Lake Mary, FL: Charisma House

D'Souza, Dinesh. *What's So Great About Christianity* (2007). Washington, DC: Regnery Publishing, Inc.

DeMar, Gary. *God and Government Volume I* (1997). Atlanta, GA: American Vision, Inc.

Doherty, Paul (1998). Victory Fellowship.

Duker-Fishman, Rivkah (April 2013). Jews in the Medieval Christian World. *Seminar for Christian Leaders.* Yad Vashem; Hebrew University, Jerusalem.

Finney, Charles. *Revivals of Religion* (1978). Virginia. CBN University Press.

Fox, Jeremy (2011). Grand Master Han Martial Arts.

Heschel, Abraham Joshua. *God in Search of Man* (1955). New York: Farrar, Straus and Giroux.

Heschel, Abraham Joshua. *The Prophets* (1999). New York: Prince Press and Hendrickson Publishers.

Idleman, Kyle *Not a Fan* (2011). Grand Rapids, MI: Zondervan.

Intrater, Keith *Covenant Relationships* (1989). Shippensburg, PA: Destiny Image Publishers

Jones, Laurie Beth *Teach Your Team to Fish* (2002). New York: Three Rivers Publishing

Lancaster, D. Thomas *King of the Jews* (2006). Littleton, CO: First Fruits of Zion, Inc.

Leal, Kevin *Jubilee Gulf Coast Conference* (2012). Pensacola, FL: Key Ministries

Len Ballenger, personal communication, 2012.

Len Ballenger, personal communication, 2013.

Len Ballenger, personal communication, 2014.

Lindell Ballenger (2011). Prosperity. Jubilee International.

Lindsley, Art *Love The Ultimate Aplogetic* (2008). Downers Grove, Illinois: IVP Books Inter Varsity Press.

Livermore, Rebecca. *Relationship Verses From The Bible And God* (Feb. 25, 2008). Yahoo! Contributor Network: Found on 24 January 2013 at http://voices.yahoo.com/relationship-verses-bible-god-1026951.html

Maier, Paul *Josephus –The Essential Works* (1988). Grand Rapids, MI: Kregel Publications.

Maimonides, Moses *The Guide of the Perplexed* (1974). Chicago, IL: University of Chicago Press.

McClendon, Trey, Press On, Jubilee International, Pensacola, FL.

Miller, Stephen M. *The Complete Guide to the Bible* (2007). Uhrichsville, OH: Barbour Publishing

Moseley, Ron *Kingdom Relationships* (2000). Clarksville, Maryland: Messianic Jewish Publishers

Moseley, Ronald W. *The Spirit and the Law* (1993).

Sherwood, AR: Mozark Research Foundation.

Moseley, Ronald W., personal communication, 2014.

Murray, Andrew. *The School of Obedience* (2002). Lewisville, TX: Accelerated Christian Education.

Nobel, David *Thinking Like a Christian* (2002). Nashville, TN: B & H Publishing.

Pratney, Winkie. *Counterfeit Conversion* (1998). Found at Ministry of Helps http://www.moh.org/WinkPrat/DTM/CounterfeitConversionPart1.htm

Roser, Phil COL (2003). Arkansas Army National Guard.

Schindler, Pesach Rabbi (April 2013). God, Jews and History. *Seminar for Christian Leaders.* Yad Vashem; Hebrew University, Jerusalem.

Silvey, Mark. *The Proverbs Plan for Family Discipleship* (2010). Parker, KS: Hearts of the Fathers.

Stanford, Miles J. *Principles for Spiritual Growth* (1982). Lincoln, NE: Back to the Bible.

Thomas, Harry (2013). Living Among Evil Doers. Fresh From Heaven Ministries.

Tolleson, William (2014). The Holy Romance. Jubilee Church International.

Valea, Earnest. *The Human Condition in World Religions* (2009). http://www.comparativereligion.com/man.htm

Vines, Paul, personal communication, 1990.

Wheeler, Douglas *Betrothed: An Intimate Face-to-Face Walk With God* (2012). Pocahontas, AR: Mended Wings Publishing.

Wheeler, Douglas, personal communication, 2014.

Wilson, J. L. (2009). *Fresh Sermons*. Fresno, CA: Willow City Press

Wilson, Marvin R. *Our Father Abraham* (1989). Grand Rapids, MI: William B. Eerdmans Publishing Company.

Young, Brad H. *Jesus The Jewish Theologian* (1995). Peabody, MA: Hendrickson Publishers

Zacharias, Ravi *Cries of the Heart* (1998). Nashville: Word Publishing.

About the Author

Pastor and Prophet Marvin Barham is senior pastor of Jubilee Church International in North Little Rock, AR which is a sister church to Jubilee Church International in Pensacola, FL under the Pastoral and Apostolic leadership of Pastor Len Ballenger. Marvin has served in ministry for over 25 years both as a youth minister, pastor, and prophet. Marvin has ministered prophetically across the country for many years with his father, Johnny Barham, and serves as Vice President of Johnny Barham Ministries. God has used him to spread the gospel and prophetic ministry throughout cities and churches in Mexico, South Africa and Brazil. He apostles' churches in Morelos and Allende, MX and Lonoke, AR. Marvin has served on the board of community ministerial alliances, as a chaplain of the Arkansas Army National Guard motorcycle club, and Vice President of the Arkansas National Guard Officers Christian Fellowship. He is a member of Highway and Hedges motorcycle ministry, Patriot riders and an Associate Staff member of Campus Crusade for Christ Military Ministry. He has served as a chaplain for GMHMA of Arkansas, and POP Warner Youth Football League. He has served as a Board Member for the Children of Arkansas Loved for a Lifetime and Co-Chair of the Arkansas Ministers Network. Marvin served over 20 years in the Arkansas Army National Guard and retired from the National Guard as a Major. He has authored and co-authored books with his father to include Understanding Your Spirit Man and the Healing of Your Soul, Operating in Your Spiritual Gifts, The Prosperity of Your Soul, The Relevance of Hebraic Idioms, Biblical Speech Communications, Who Am I children's book and many others. He ministers in the areas of preaching, teaching, healing, prophetic ministry, praise and worship and inspirational fine art. He preaches from a Hebraic perspective with prophetic revelation. Marvin carries a strong passion for saving the lost, discipling the nations, and feeding God's sheep with the uncompromising Word of Truth. He operates in personal and corporate prophetic ministry. He teaches in the areas of leadership, prophetic instruction, Hebraic concepts, inspirational painting, music and much more. God has placed on his heart a desire to see the restoration of the New Testament church and the Voice of God carried throughout the earth. Marvin holds a BA from the University of Arkansas at Little Rock, Masters of Religious Education (M.R.E.) and Middle Eastern Studies from the American Institute for Advanced Biblical Studies, and a Doctorate of Ministry (D. Min) from Jubilee College International. He has also studied Holocaust History and sat under Professors from Hebrew University at the Yad Vashim Institute in Jerusalem, Israel. He has ministered in diverse denominations to include Baptist, Presbyterian, Methodist, and Messianic congregations. He is a sought after speaker and continues a national and international traveling ministry in addition to his oversight of Jubilee College International School of Ministry (A satellite campus of Jubilee College International). He and his wife Angie have been married 24 years and have home schooled their five children.

Building Your Love Story

Other Books by Dr. Marvin Barham

Operating in Your Spiritual Gifts by Marvin Barham (Jun 12, 2013)
$3.99 Kindle Purchase
Auto-delivered wirelessly

Prime members read for free Join Amazon Prime
Books: See all 9 items

Operating in Your Spiritual Gifts by Dr. Marvin R. Barham (Mar 21, 2013)
$17.00 $10.80 Paperback *Prime*
Order in the next 20 hours and get it by Monday, May 19
More Buying Choices - Paperback
$8.57 new (13 offers)
$12.70 used (7 offers)

FREE Shipping on orders over $35
Books: See all 9 items

Understanding Your Spirit Man and the healing of your soul by Johnny R. Barham and Marvin R. Barham (Aug 9, 2004)
$3.99 Kindle Edition
Auto-delivered wirelessly

Books: See all 9 items

The Relevance of Hebraic Idioms: In Post-Modern English Speaking Cultures by Marvin R. Barham (Aug 30, 2010)
$12.00 $9.50 Paperback *Prime*
Order in the next 12 hours and get it by Monday, May 19
More Buying Choices - Paperback
$9.50 new (3 offers)
$38.24 used (5 offers)

FREE Shipping on orders over $35
Books: See all 9 items

Understanding Your Spirit Man and the healing of your soul by Marvin Barham (Aug 11, 2004)
$17.50 $15.75 Paperback *Prime*
Order in the next 20 hours and get it by Monday, May 19
More Buying Choices - Paperback
$15.11 new (9 offers)
$15.00 used (5 offers)

FREE Shipping on orders over $35
Books: See all 9 items

Prosperity by Marvin Barham (Jun 12, 2013)
$3.99 Kindle Purchase
Auto-delivered wirelessly
$12.00 $11.40 Paperback *Prime*
Order in the next 12 hours and get it by Monday, May 19

Prime members read for free Join Amazon Prime

Who Am I by Marvin R. Barham (May 12, 2011)
$19.28 $10.40 Paperback *Prime*
Order in the next 12 hours and get it by Monday, May 19
More Buying Choices - Paperback
$39.49 used (4 offers)

FREE Shipping on orders over $35
Books: See all 9 items

Speech Communications Instructors Manual (Volume 1) by Dr Marvin R. Barham (Feb 29, 2012)
$19.95 **$18.96** Paperback
Order in the next 12 hours and get it by Monday, May 13
FREE Shipping on orders over $35
Books: See all 9 items

Speech Communications Student Workbook (Volume 1) by Dr Marvin R. Barham (Feb 29, 2012)
$16.50 **$15.16** Paperback
Order in the next 12 hours and get it by Monday, May 13
FREE Shipping on orders over $35
Books: See all 9 items

For more information or to book Dr. Barham at your next event visit us at www.marvinbarham.org.

Made in the USA
Monee, IL
30 March 2022